Contents

Introduction

It was several years ago when some impactful experiences of mine were laying heavy on my mind, giving me the idea to write. I was in my thirties and the thought of parents discouraging their kids from following their dreams was inspiring me to share my story with others. I felt like parents tried to push their kids into the areas of their own failed dreams. In my case, I wanted my son to grow up and play professional basketball because that was what I really wanted to do when I was growing up; it was my own, never-achieved dream. My motivation to write was to bridge the gap between parents and children so that children could feel free to chase their dreams, even if it seemed crazy or outlandish. At the time I had a professional writer helping me and quickly had a few chapters under my belt. Fast forward twenty years, and after going through a divorce, I was not in the place to write this book. I was still processing and understanding that some of my failures in life were tied to my rough childhood and a lack of my father being there for me.

My purpose for this book is to uncover the deep connection between the patterned hardships of adult men to the relationships they had with their fathers growing up. So many men in this world that have struggled in life, whether in their relationships with their wives and children or with a failed business, have also struggled during their childhood and upbringing. Little boys look up to their dads and desire to grow up to be as strong as them one day. One thing that these little boys can't see, is these grown men are little boys too, still struggling with their own difficult childhood. The sad thing is that a lot of dads will repeat the same mistakes in raising their sons just as their dad raised them. It may not be intentional because it is a subconsciously learned behavior. If it isn't recognized, then the cycle cannot be broken.

I will share many stories in this book that I feel will help fathers and sons all over the world receive healing and understand why they instinctively parent the way that they do.

Many tears have been shed in the writing of this book. Writing has pulled so many emotions out of me that are difficult to experience. My wife would come home and see me shaking and crying from the pain. She would tell me not to cry, but I needed to in order to experience some healing from my screwed-up childhood.

My parents never divorced, and my dad was in the house throughout my whole childhood, but he was absent as a father. There are a lot of kids raised in broken homes of divorced parents where the fathers left and were never involved in their kids' lives either. I find that in both scenarios, the kids are affected the same way emotionally, but not financially since it is harder for a single mom to raise her kids without financial support from the father. Boys need love and affirmation from their dads. If they don't receive it as a child, then it will affect them in their everyday life.

In my twenties and thirties, I was trying to prove to the world that I was important. I desired people to recognize the talents that I had. I was insecure about who I was, and I tried to be somebody I wasn't. I would make my life sound better than it actually was because I was not comfortable in my own skin. In my forties, I began to understand the way that I was portraying myself. I started to own up to my failures instead of blaming my dad for everything. I was very bitter towards my dad even after he had passed, and granted, I had justification for being that way. At some point, you have to stop playing the victim role and rise above your problems to be victorious. We love to blame the past for our problems when in the future, but it only keeps us from moving forward in our lives and from being the person that God intends for us to be. I know I would not be the dad, husband, grandfather, or coach that I am today if I continued to blame my past and remained a victim.

I hope this book will help you to overcome your past and change your life for the positive. Writing this book has challenged me and changed me as a person. I have received healing from the deep scars of my childhood by writing this book. As a coach, I realized that I need to be a father figure to the kids on my team that are fatherless by providing direction and support, building them up, encouraging them, and inspiring them to be great in life.

I want to thank my wife for being a support to me in the writing of this book. She has been a rock in our relationship and has helped me remove the excuses from my life. Now, instead of saying I can't do something, I say to myself I can do anything I put my mind to. I pray that this book will be a blessing to you. Thank you for taking the time to read this book.

Chapter One

The Father I Never Knew

"Hear, ye children, the instruction of a father, and attend to know understanding," (Proverbs 4:1). Boys all over the world naturally look to their fathers for instruction, protection, and direction. Fathers struggle daily to find direction for their own lives, never mind trying to give direction to their sons. Whether they never received proper direction from their fathers or they are so consumed with their own problems, fathers fall short of leading their sons onto the right path and setting an honored example. Direction was a necessity that my dad never received from his. My grandfather, although a great guy, was always consumed with work. It stole precious and crucial time away from his family. Because of my grandfather's busy work schedule, my dad was the one who took care of his four younger sisters growing up.

My grandmother was never the nurturing type. Instead, she was the disciplinarian in the family. My grandfather was easy-going and fun to be around. I was always excited when he came over, but if my grandma came with him, I was not happy. She would exert authority and constantly tried to tell us what to do. I hated being told what to do, especially by my grandma. I would talk back to her and tell her that she couldn't tell me what to do because she wasn't my mom. I wasn't always very respectful as a kid and was also a little rebellious.

I never saw my dad and grandma hug each other or show affection to one another at all. My dad only called my grandma by her first name, Martha. I never understood why my dad wouldn't call her 'mom'. I assumed that something bad must have happened during his childhood to make him call her Martha. My dad never talked about his upbringing and refused to explain why he called his mom by her first name. Sometimes if I was on the phone with my dad, I would try to question him about it. He would avoid my curiosity and threaten to hang up on me if I kept asking him about it. Not being explained this unusual interaction between my grandmother and dad only made me more eager to know, so I would beg him for an explanation. Then, click. He would hang up on me because I wanted answers.

My dad did not receive the nurture that is supposed to be given from a mom or the guidance that should be shown from a dad. For my father, this was a recipe for disaster when it came to raising kids, especially sons. From the outside looking in, we had the perfect home life. We lived in a three-bedroom house with a finished basement and a pool in the backyard. Our house was in a nice neighborhood and all our neighbors were like family. On almost every major holiday we always had neighborhood parties (Memorial Day, 4th of July, Labor Day, etc.). My dad was the life of the party, especially when he was drinking. He told jokes all night long and my neighbors absolutely loved it. Everyone probably thought I was so lucky to have such a funny man as my dad, but life was not fun at home. He was good at pretending and putting on a show to make it seem like we were a happy and loving household. The only time that my dad ever told me he loved me was when we were coming home from a party. He was drunk in the back seat when he looked at me and said, "Leo, I love you." I was completely shocked. I remember telling myself that he was only saying that to me because he was drunk.

Life at our house wasn't anything close to the fake show put on when others were around. My dad always came home from work in a bad mood. Instead of telling jokes, he would just yell at everyone. It was like Dr. Jekyll and Mr. Hyde- two completely different people. One was the funny guy at the party that everyone loved to be around, and the other was a mean bully, throwing insults around the house as if it was his best contribution to the family. It was miserable whenever my dad was home. As soon as we heard him pull in the driveway, we all scattered like field mice being chased by a cat. There wasn't ever a joyful greeting at the door with excitement that dad was home. Instead, we would say, "Crap! Dad is home. Let's get to the basement so we don't have to see him." We isolated from him in the basement but would have to resurface for dinner.

We always ate dinner together every night. You would think the daily ritual of eating together as a family would be nice, right? No. It was awful.

To be honest, dinner time was the toughest time of the day for me. If I wasn't home, my dad would whistle for me to come home and if I didn't come home right away, then I would be in big trouble and maybe even grounded. There was no flexibility. Dinner was at five. We were expected to be there by five and not a minute later. For most families, dinner is a time to hear about everyone's day, laugh, joke around, and enjoy spending time with one another. The Hilton house was not like that though. We were lucky enough to get to listen to my dad bitch about life, his kids, and my mom's cooking. Even though my mom worked very hard every single night to make dinner for the entire family, my dad would religiously criticize her cooking. I can still remember the mean and hateful comments about her cooking coming from that man. I would practically inhale my food so that I could get the hell away from him before he could start bitching at me next. Out of my three siblings, my sister had it the worst at dinner time. My sister is the oldest and has down syndrome. Although my dad fought for her to have the same rights as the other kids at school, he was so mean to her, especially at dinner. He would make fun of her for the way she ate her food. Most down syndrome kids are very happy and usually in a good mood, but my sister was not a happy person. She was moody and always had a frown on her face. She would become emotionally unstable at times from the stress of our home life. Watching my dad make fun of her about how she ate her food made me so angry. I became determined that when I got bigger, I was going to stand up to him and put an end to his unbearable madness.

The only relief I had every night was when my dad went upstairs after dinner to take a nap. Some nights he would have to go back to work at his ceramic shop to teach pottery classes. Those nights were the best. When he left, the house would come alive with laughter and excitement. It was like a completely different world inside our house. Everyone's shields would disappear. The energy would shift from fear to peaceful freedom. We would literally let out a sigh of relief knowing that it was safe to be ourselves again. Without our dad around, we were able to enjoy playing board games, baking cookies with our mom, and watching movies together. Watching a movie with my dad meant absolutely no talking, no laughing, and no having fun. Retreating to the basement when he came home was a natural force of habit. The energy shift that occurred as soon as he walked through those doors at night was crazy.

As a kid, I would dream of a world without my dad in it. What a shame it is for a child to feel that way about their father. I consistently wished for my mom to leave my dad. In my opinion, it would have been better for all of us if she did. She threatened to leave him several times, but it never happened. I think it's because she believed that she wouldn't be able to support us by herself. I wouldn't have cared if we were homeless under a bridge if I didn't have to see my dad anymore. I would have been happier without him in my life. I was the youngest of four watching each of my siblings take his abuse. I remember thinking that once I was big enough, I was not going to let him get away with his verbal abuse anymore. His hatefulness was creating a ticking time bomb inside of me. The anger was growing day by day.

Proverbs 22:6 says to train up a child in the way he should go, and he will not depart from it. We didn't receive any training in our house of any kind from our dad. The provocation from my dad created so much anger and frustration in our lives. He didn't take the time to give us direction. Not having a dad that truly loved and cared for me impacted my life in negative ways, from early childhood to being a grown adult.

I became a Christian at the age of 17. The church says becoming a Christian gives you a completely new life, allowing the old things to perish for good. This is very true in a lot of ways, but I really struggled with the concept of moving past the trauma from my dad. The wounds were too deep to be healed or forgotten overnight. The anger and bitterness inside of me were a strong-rooted tree that was infecting my whole life. It was incomprehensible for me to obtain the Faith that my problems were suddenly solved. The resentment I had of my father grew more when I read the bible and learned about the expectations and purposes of a father. It made me realize how my dad wasn't even close to being anything like the dad he was supposed to be. This man was my father and yet, I didn't even know who he was, nor did I care to know either. He was more of a stranger than he was a father. I wanted my dad to be my hero, role model, and someone to look up to. Unfortunately, it was the complete opposite. I've always said that when I have kids I will love them, support them, and guide them towards becoming a success in their lives.

When I make mistakes as a dad, I apologize to my kids and try to be open and honest with them. I want them to feel connected with me. They will know my strengths and weaknesses. Fatherless sons are a huge dilemma in the world today. Whether they are absent from the home or just uninvolved fathers in the house like my dad was. The repercussions can be felt in our society today from kids dropping out of high school and turning to drugs and crime, eventually ending up in our prisons. Fatherless sons become fathers themselves and end up repeating the cycle.

Being a father is a tough job, especially if you didn't have a great dad to be an example for you. My dad was never easy to approach. Trying to have a regular conversation with him was intimidating, so asking him for permission to do something was awful. Every time I asked my dad if I could do something, the answer was always no. I became defiant and sneaky since he never let me do anything. I decided that I would do what I wanted to do, and nobody was going to control me or try to tell me no. I would always ask my mom for permission first, but she would tell me to ask my dad and see what he says first. I knew he was just going to say no, so why bother? Even if I asked permission for something as simple as going to my friend's house, he would say no. I realized at a young age that it was better for me to ask for forgiveness rather than permission. Still to this day, I can't stand it when someone tells me no or says that I can't do something.

I remember really wanting a skateboard once, but I knew that my dad would tell me I couldn't have one. So, I decided to buy one anyway and hid it under my bed. It took about a year for my dad to even find out about it. As I said, it was better to ask for forgiveness instead of permission. My mom knew about the skateboard, but she never told my dad. Most of the time when I was asking my mom for permission to do something, she would cave under the pressure of me bugging the tar out of her. She let me do some things that my dad wouldn't have approved of, and she kept it a secret from him too. Whenever he would find out about me doing something without his permission or knowledge, my mom would usually stick up for me.

When I was nine years old, I started delivering newspapers so that I could make my own money. The paper route was passed down to me from my brothers. I wanted my independence bad and this way I could finally buy the things that I wanted to without the permission of my parents. Eventually, I was able to buy a snowmobile with my own money that I had saved from my paper route. My dad was fine with us having snowmobiles, but motorcycles were not allowed at our house. For some reason my dad hated motorcycles, but I loved them. So, guess what my next purchase was? You guessed it, a motorcycle. I was thirteen when I bought my first dirt bike and I loved riding it. You're probably wondering how I kept it hidden from my dad. Well, I hid it in our shed where we kept our snowmobiles because my dad practically never went out there. I only rode it whenever my dad wasn't home or when he was upstairs taking a nap. I had to sneak it in and out of the yard, constantly trying to keep that part of my life hidden from him.

One day during the summer my brother and I were working on the motorcycle in the backyard when my dad unexpectedly came home for lunch. I remember thinking, Crap! Dad is home. I never thought that he would come home for lunch but boy was I wrong. He was pissed when he saw us with the motorcycle. He asked us who it belonged to, and I told him that it was mine.

"You are going to sell this," he said to me.

I snapped back, "No, I am not. I paid for it with my own money, and I am keeping it."

"Ok," he said, "Then I am calling the cops on you."

"Go ahead." Then I took off on it as he was yelling at me.

When I came home later, he did not say a single thing to me about any of it at all. I ended up selling the bike later on and bought an even bigger motorcycle. My dad didn't seem to care about that either.

I was definitely different from my brothers in the way that my attitude was. I always behaved like I was going to do what I wanted to do, and nobody was going to tell me anything different. I know I was defiant and rebellious towards my dad, but it was my way of coping through the tough times as a teenager living in that house. Not all kids with attitudes and are disrespectful are bad kids. There were reasons why I was the way that I was, and my dad had a lot to do with it. Not being allowed to be adventurous as a boy impacted me a great deal. Even though my dad always tried to control me and keep me from expressing myself, he did not have the best of luck doing so.

I think it is important for us as dads to think about the ways that our dads raised us. Take note of both the good things and the bad things. See what needs changing in the ways that we are a father to our sons. Any negative patterns that we have learned from our fathers shouldn't be passed down. It's crazy that it's easier to parent our kids when they are young and dependent on us, but when they start to get older and are in their teenage years it gets so much harder. Their teenage years are when they challenge our authority and our position as their dad. They try to push the boundaries and see what they can get away with. We must be careful with the ways we navigate our relationship with our sons. We don't want to be on autopilot and react abruptly whenever a problem arises. We must be proactive and remain interested in what they are going through. We need to be able to help them avoid pitfalls in their lives. I think we all know that we are not perfect, even when we are trying to do the best job that we can possibly do as a father. If we can be happy with ourselves and be with our sons, then the relationship will develop deep roots that will last forever, even after we are gone.

Chapter Two:

Defiant Child

For as long as I can remember, I was always a scrappy child. Looking back, fighting with my two older brothers helped mold me into a strong and determined kid. I had two older brothers. One was six years older than me, and the other was four years older than me. They always seemed to be in cahoots with each other whenever it came to picking on me. They would call me a brat and say that I was always bothering them, and to be fair, they were definitely right to some degree. I used to try to take them both on at the same time, I did not come out as the winner, and then continue coming at them for more. No matter how hard they knocked me down, I would still get right back up and go at them again for more abuse. I would frequently end up in a headlock with my underwear pulled over my head while receiving a noogie, yet I would continue to fight them. I was relentless. I would keep bugging them, repeatedly asking for more abuse, regardless of how badly I was getting whipped. One day, my older brother Ed and I were fighting when I sucker-punched him in the gut and made him cry. He went and told my parents, and they grounded me for hitting him. It was the best day of my life. I remember feeling proud and not minding that I was in trouble at all that day. My older brothers definitely taught me to be tough and not back down from anyone. Sparring with my older brothers helped prepare me to stand up to my dad when he verbally abused my mother.

Not only was I a scrappy kid, but I also had a lot of anger built up from the way my dad treated all of us. It was hard for me to watch my neighbor's dads be so supportive of their sons by coaching their teams or being their scout leaders. I was so jealous of them and even more relentless towards my dad because of it. It felt unfair to me that my dad was mean and critical, and their dads were uplifting and encouraging. I had a chip on my shoulder, making me think that it was me against the world and I could not take shit from anyone. I'm in my fifties now, and I still feel like it's me against the world. It is such a crazy thing. Sometimes I feel as if I am banging my head against the wall, still trying to be defiant in my life, with a constant need to be in competition with absolutely everyone in every way imaginable. Living life like this is hard and debilitatingly exhausting. I am still working through this instinctive mindset so that one day I won't feel like I have to be this way. Even with silly things like racing other cars and trying to get in front of them while I'm driving. The other cars don't even know that I am racing them, yet I have created this competition. It's crazy and funny to me at the same time. While I am writing this book, I am seeing why I am like this. I always found affirmation in the competitions I won in any sport or game. Even fights I was involved in and won would make me feel proud and strong. When I didn't win, I would feel devastated and like a failure.

In my younger days, I got into many fights with kids at my elementary school. If someone made me mad, I would fight them in an instant. I didn't care about how much bigger or stronger anyone was compared to me. I was considered the toughest kid in my grade because I had a bad attitude and was not afraid to fight anyone. Sometimes, a healthy fear can keep you out of trouble. The rage inside me did not make me think about the repercussions of my actions. As a result of my short fuse, I spent a significant amount of time in the principal's office. The principal was a black belt, which made a lot of kids afraid of getting into trouble and being sent to his office, but it didn't scare me or even phase me at all. I was considered a bully in elementary school for two reasons: 1.) I fought a lot. And 2.) I picked on kids at times to make me feel better about myself. People were either scared of me or just didn't like me, so having friends was tough for me. By the time I was in middle school, I had calmed down a lot. I was involved in school sports and had an outlet for my anger. Despite my reputation, I was only suspended once for fighting in school. My lacrosse coach was very upset with me for fighting. My parents were called in for a meeting with my coach and teacher. That was not a fun day for me to have to sit in front of my parents, my coach, and my teacher. Not only was I suspended from school for a day, but I also had to sit out for one game. This motivated me to not fight anymore because I loved sports and did not want to miss out on any games that we played.

Before writing this book, I never truly understood why I was so obsessed with sports, but thoroughly looking back on my timeline of life has unblurred quite a few connections. My great escape from the toxic environment at home was getting out of the house and playing sports with the neighborhood kids. Naturally, it was an opportunity for me to blow off some steam. Being yelled at constantly without any good reason made me one angry kid with quite some rage. I used all of that built-up energy to be a dominator in sports. Some kids in the neighborhood wouldn't even want to play with me because of how rough and aggressive I would be to win. I excelled in every sport that I played, whether it was baseball, basketball, football, lacrosse, soccer, hockey, tennis, or racquetball. As long as I practiced just a little bit, I was a strong athlete and a challenging competitor in any sport. The amount of time I spent playing sports shaped me to take my athletic performance seriously. I remember my neighbors saying that I was always playing some kind of sport whenever they saw me. I believe God used it to keep me from getting into trouble and possibly going down the wrong path. Playing sports was my refuge.

I started lifting weights when I was in the fifth grade, and my motivation wasn't to improve my skills in sports or my athleticism. Working towards the day that I would finally be able to stop my dad from yelling at my mom and everyone else in my family is what motivated me. My goal was to be stronger than my dad. I was determined to rescue my mom from his verbal abuse. It was disturbing to wake up every day and hear my dad yell at my mom, criticizing her for everything she was doing wrong in her life. By the time I reached the eighth grade, I had really developed into a strong athlete. My basketball coach would always joke about making a boxer out of me because of how highly inclined I was to brawl. He knew how rough things were with my dad at home. When my coach would pick me up for practice, he would always ask me how Dickie was doing, meaning my dad, whose name was Richard but went by Dick for short. As a kid, I thought it was the perfect name for him since he always acted like a dick to his family. I would respond to my coach by saying that he was still being a dick, and we would both chuckle. At the time, it was a stress reliever for me to laugh about it, but now I don't find it very funny. I now have sympathy for my dad. As an adult, I understand that my dad had unresolved issues stemming from his childhood that were never handled even in his adulthood.

My basketball coach was also my best friend's dad. I spent a lot of time at my best friend's house, and his dad would try to comfort me with the encouragement that everything would be alright. One of the saddest things I went through as a kid was when my coach was diagnosed with cancer. He passed away later that year. We were only in the eighth grade. It was super tough watching my friend and his whole family go through the pain of losing a wonderful father and husband. We used to call him Coach Sal because his name was Salvatore. I always looked up to him and viewed him as a father figure. He consistently worked with my best friend and my best friend's brother for hours in their driveway, training them to become incredible basketball players. After his death, their motivation to practice basketball diminished. They still loved the game, but their drive wasn't there as much after losing their biggest cheerleader and supporter. Despite their passion diminishing, they still excelled in the sport because of their dad's solid foundation he built for them. But without Coach Sal, a part of me always felt that they could have achieved so much more if their dad was still alive during their playing days in high school.

After my coach passed away, I spent many days at my friends' house. I almost lived there. It was insanely different without his dad watching basketball on TV with us or playing hoops in the driveway with us. I always looked forward to going over to my best friend's house and escaping the misery at my house, so you can imagine that losing a coach who was like a father to me was tough. It was excruciating for my best friend and his family to go through it. Seeing their pain was also rough.

My father's neglect and absence are why I am passionate about coaching sports. I always looked at coaches as father figures and mentors growing up. Now I can impact kids who might not have close relationships with their dads or who might not have a dad in their lives at all. I know from my own experience that building confidence in a sport can translate into other areas of life.

My dad never established confidence in my life, so I independently poured all of my time into sports and working out. I wanted to be the best at every sport I played, so I would practice for hours. Even in the middle of a sport's season, I would play off-season sports. I once sprained my ankle playing basketball during lacrosse season, and my lacrosse coach was pretty upset with me. He was yelling at me, "Hilton! It is lacrosse season. Do not play any sport besides lacrosse during our season."

When I first started playing sports in my younger years, I longed for my dad to be at my games. When I got older, I didn't want him at any of my games because of how angry I was at him. Deep down inside, I longed for a dad who cheered me on while watching me play, someone who would give me advice after the games and tell me what I could improve on. The reality would hit when I came home from my games. My dad could give two shits about how I did at my games or if I won. The desire for a dad that was there when I was little to say, "Leo, let's shoot hoops so you can work on your game to get better." I strongly wished to have a dad like that when I was younger. I would tell myself that I would be the kind of dad that played sports with his kids and invested his time and energy into their

interests.

At a very young age, I was determined not to repeat the cycle, and at age 51, I can say I am proud that I have broken the cycle. I remember when I came home from elementary school and told my dad that I was going to play in the NBA one day. He shot my dreams down immediately and told me that it was impossible for me. The funny thing is that I used to play against some NBA players when I was in my twenties, and I could compete on the same level as them too. Not having my dad encourage me caused bitterness to grow inside me. My high school lacrosse team was also number one in the nation for several years. In seventh grade, I was determined to get a scholarship to Syracuse University to play lacrosse. My dad shot me down again and said there was no way I could do that. He had this smirk on his face and laughed as he said it. Kids have dreams, and when you shoot them down, it causes deep roots of bitterness in their hearts. At this point, my anger was getting out of control. Not only was my dad constantly yelling at my mom and everyone else in the house, but he was wrecking the dreams I had in my life too.

I was determined to stand up to the injustice and protect myself from the verbal assault. There were times that I wanted to run away, but I loved my mom and did not want to leave her because I felt that I needed to protect her. My mom would try to talk to me and say, "Leo, your dad loves you. He just doesn't know how to show it." I would laugh at her. "Really, mom? He sure has a funny way of showing his love." As you can tell, I was not buying it. But I believe that my mom's love kept me from losing my mind and killing my dad. I have to say that where my dad lacked in showing love to all of us, my mom made up for it with the love that she offered. She sacrificed for us and gave up things in her own life just for us.

Moms are great at nurturing, showing love, and providing comfort, but they cannot take the place of an absent father. I do hear the stories of the moms who stepped up, delivered discipline, and filled the dad's role in the home. I genuinely do not think we understand the damage done to boys when their dads are not there to give them affirmation and direction in their lives. The dads with their sons' backs give them so much courage in their journey that it instills this fire inside them that allows them to do absolutely anything. Even when they face something that scares them, they always have their supportive father there for them to say, "You go, boy! You can accomplish anything. I believe in you!" Sometimes, having somebody who believes in your dreams more than you helps you achieve them, even when you have doubts. I have done that with my sons at certain times in their lives. It does not matter how old they are, either. My 31-year-old son has a side business and wants to quit his full-time job to have more time to spend working on it. He has reservations about taking that step, but I told him to go for it because the reward could be enormous. I told him to trust in his talent and himself; he can do it, and he can do it well. You must believe in your kids' dreams, not try to deter them and tell them all the reasons why it might not work. Don't be the negative Nelly in your kids' lives.

The bond between a father and son is unique, just like the bond between a mother and daughter. As a good father, you long for your kids to be more successful than you are and accomplish things that you couldn't. You worry about every stage of your son's life, no matter how old he is. You hope that they avoid the same pitfalls you fell into as a young adult. My other son is doing very well working in Indiana. When he first told me he had taken a job in a different state, I was shocked. He had always lived at home with us, even throughout college. My daughter has traveled the world, so I would have expected it from her, but not from my son. I was excited for him to move to Indiana and start his new job, but I was also very nervous. Deep down inside, I knew it would be good for him to get out of the nest we had created for him in our home. The night before he moved into his apartment, we slept in the same room at an Airbnb, and I could feel his nerves. He was keeping me awake from breathing so heavily. When we woke up the following morning, I was determined to make his apartment feel warm and inviting, just like his room was at our house. My daughter and I spent all day buying stuff and decorating the apartment for him to make it his new home. We had dinner there, played cards, laughed, and had a good time in his new home. That Sunday was tough because I had to leave to go back to Atlanta. I cried almost the whole way home. My daughter comforted me by saying, "Dad, it's going to be all right. He's got this." I knew that he would be successful, but the reality of it was emotional.

It made me think back to when I moved from my childhood home in Syracuse to Chicago. I was his age when I packed my truck up, and my dad couldn't have cared less. I think he said goodbye to me, but I cannot remember. I felt like there was that 'don't let the door hit you on the way out' attitude. He was probably happy that I was leaving because it didn't seem to faze him. On the other hand, my mom hugged me. She was sad when I moved out for the first time. She was always such a support in my life, no matter what I was doing. Being with my son during his move made me believe that my dad missed out on an opportunity to be involved in my life. He had completely disregarded a chance to be close to his son.

Seeing my kids grow up and be successful is an incredible feeling. My son moved back to Atlanta during the coronavirus because his contract had ended and they did not renew it. They asked him if he would move back for another contract three months later. I was shocked again when he decided to take the job. At the time, I was swamped and didn't think I would be able to go with him to help find an apartment, but I was willing to take the time if I had to. He said to me, Dad, I can do this on my own, and I want to do it on my own." I told him that I had confidence that he could do this independently. Letting go as a parent is not easy. It was tough seeing him pack up the car and leave without me, but he did a great job finding an apartment. My little boy has become a man, and I am so proud of the man that he is today.

Seeing my kids grow up and become successful adults is a rewarding feeling. It can also be challenging to realize that they don't need you as much anymore. It can create a space once filled by an act of caring for your child. But I sure don't miss them asking me for money all the time. Maybe that's why you have more money in your fifties and sixties. Knowing that I did a great job as a dad to my sons is gratifying. It brings a feeling of accomplishment to be an example of how a father should be to their sons so that they will make great dads to their own, especially to their sons. As I write this book, the wounds still run deep from how I missed out on having a father who invested in my life. Oh, how different my life would be if I had a great relationship with my dad. The struggle is real for men who did not have a relationship with their dads growing up. This defiant child has grown into a man with deep wounds. I have my doubts that they will ever heal.

As dads, we must be careful not to create anger and bitterness in our sons. We cannot impose our failed dreams. Saying you want your son to be a doctor, lawyer, or professional athlete is very specific and could be toxic to the relationship. Let them follow their dreams, even if they seem weird or far-fetched to you. We need to support them and encourage them to go after their dreams. We need to instill the belief that if they work hard and believe in themselves, they can achieve anything they want. Don't dismiss them or try to point them in a different direction; just be there for them and help them keep going after their dreams. We cannot clip their wings for them to stay sheltered in our home. We have to release them from their nest and help them fly to achieve their dreams.

I named my son Leo Tyrone Hilton because I thought it would sound good being announced at the United Center as he was coming out for the Chicago Bulls lineup. That was my dream, not his. Today, my son is not in the NBA but is a mechanical engineer with a minor in aerospace engineering. I am prouder of his academic achievements than if he had made it to the NBA. Maybe because the only A I ever received in high school was in gym class. I was a B and C student in high school, maybe borderline D. I never applied myself in school. But I was sure proud of how hard my son would work in college to finish his degrees. So, make sure you encourage your sons to chase after their dreams. You want your sons to look back later in life and be able to say that their dad was always their biggest fan, no matter what they did.

Chapter 3:

The Words of My Father
(Daggers to My Heart for a Lifetime)

Sticks and stones may break your bones, but words can never hurt you. This is the biggest lie of all time. I grew up with that saying. It was probably intended to keep kids from reacting to name-calling with violence. Still, I got into many fights over somebody calling me or my family names. You can heal from sticks and stones, but you may never recover from the negative words spoken to you over your lifetime. I am a grandfather, and the negative comments from my father still affect me today.

Proverbs 15:4: Gentle words bring life and health but a deceitful tongue crushes the spirit.

Proverbs 16:24: Kind words are like honey sweet to the soul and healthy for the body.

Proverbs 18:4: A person's words can be life giving water words of true wisdom are as refreshing as a bubbling brook.

So, in the Bible, Proverbs clearly teaches the importance of the words we speak to each other and the power they have to build up or tear down. The things we say are incredibly impactful when speaking to our sons as fathers. Sometimes when my wife and I are out to dinner, we hear parents talking negatively to their kids about how they can't ever do anything right. We've witnessed parents publicly scolding their children with insults like stupid, crybaby, and dummy. It saddens me because those words will stick with them for a long time, like daggers to the heart. Given children's imaginations and creative minds, we can't destroy them with our negative talk. Verbal abuse can create an identity crisis later in life. That is why I have not told many people about my writing of this book. I do not want to hear people's negative opinions, even though I am sure I would get some positive responses too.

My dad was never that person with encouraging compliments. I never heard anything close to, "Leo, you are so smart, talented, and a great athlete." Instead, it was always, "You're an idiot. Why are you so stupid? You will never amount to anything." If I had any dreams about my future growing up, my dad would always shoot me down. So anything I've accomplished in my life has always been with the words in my head telling me that I'm not smart enough or good enough. The good thing about me is that regardless of the constant doubt and discouragement, I have always been crazy enough to try new things anyway.

In my 52 years of life, I have accomplished a lot. But no matter what it is, from getting Employee of the Month to Coach of the Year in the State of Georgia to earning my pilot's license afterward, there is a letdown for me. I am trying so hard in my life to show people that I am worth something. Because I never received words of affirmation from my father or heard him say how proud he was of me. That would have made an enormous difference in my life, even now as a man who just turned 52. I remember the day I received my Employee of the Month award. I was out in the field and got a page to come back to the office for a meeting. Remember the pager days? I thought I was in trouble or that something was wrong with the job that I was doing. It turns out the meeting was about me winning Employee of the Month.

I used to work as a personal trainer at a high-end club in Chicago. Michael Jordan and his family were members here. I had only been working there a few weeks when my supervisor called and asked me to meet her in her office. I was thinking, "Oh crap, what did I do wrong now?" I was in the process of starting a basketball program at the club. The first thing she said to me when I walked in was, "Leo, we have to make this basketball program work." I was like, "Why, what's wrong?" She informed me that Michael Jordan's kids were the first to sign up for the program. No pressure at all for me. I thought, "Why would the best basketball player in the world want me to teach his kids how to play basketball?" The club's program was a big success, and I surprised myself.

I had to block out those negative words that would always be in my head so that I could take risks and try new things to be successful in my life. Nelson Mandela once quoted the words of the poet William Earnest Henley: "I am the master of my fate and the captain of my soul." He had been in prison in South Africa for probably a lifetime, and he was telling people that he would be the President of South Africa one day. The guards would laugh at him, mock him, ask him to stop dreaming, and tell him that he would never leave this prison. Nelson also said, "Do not judge me by my successes, but by how many times I fell down and got back up again." Here he was in prison for rising up against the government for the unjust treatment of people of color. He still held on to the vision of a society free from prejudice and racism. There is great power in those who believe in themselves and their dreams, no matter how many times they fail or fall down. Despite the many people telling them they cannot achieve their dreams, they do. Nelson Mandela was released from prison, but I do not think he was ever in jail because he envisioned himself free all the time. He became president of South Africa and was never bitter toward his captors. He forgave them and knew it was all part of God's plan.

I have spent my life trying to pour positive messages into myself from Jim Rohn, Tony Robbins, Joe Vitale, Zig Zigler, and Bob Proctor, to name a few. Don't get me wrong; I believe the books and videos have helped me a lot, but there is still a deep, nagging wound in my heart from childhood that flares up from time to time. This debilitating doubt can sometimes take a little bit for me to shake off. All it takes is for my really busy boss to not return my call, and I will feel like I did something wrong, or he probably thinks I am not doing a good job. It could be if I make a mistake, and it can rattle my confidence. It is like indigestion; it just rears its head at bad times. Overall, I have worked hard to change the way I think, but the scars are deep, and I am not sure if they will ever go away. I believe it is God's way of using the tough times in our childhood to keep us humble and to depend on him and not ourselves. He is vital in our weakness if we let go and let God take control. Easier said than done.

Proverbs 18:21 says "Words kill or words give life: there is either poison or fruit."

Fathers, when raising your children, you must choose your words wisely. The terms we use will help shape our boys into the men we envision for them. They are like a rudder on a ship that could guide them to a bright future or an end of rough seas. So guard your tongue and ensure you speak words of affirmation and encouragement.

How about King David, who was chosen to be the King of Israel, but when the prophet came to Jesse's house (David's father) to anoint one of his sons to be the next King, he only brought out 7 sons, of which he has 8. The prophet said it was none of them and asked if he had any more sons. He said he had another son, but he knew it was not the one. He takes care of the sheep. The prophet says, "Bring him to me." The dad is reluctant but does it anyway. Yes, he is the next king. The dad and his other sons are shocked. What does this say about the dad's confidence in his son? David was the least favorite of Jesse's sons, yet God chose him. We need to have confidence in our sons as fathers. David rose to the challenge; he believed in himself. I mean, he had been out in the fields fighting off bears and wolves; he was not scared. You all know the story of David against Goliath—the underdog who takes down the giant when nobody would step up because they were afraid. This little shepherd boy was so petite and skinny that he couldn't wear the armor they gave him.

He did become the next king, but King Saul was so jealous of David that he chased him and tried to kill him. David spent a long time hiding out in caves and fleeing King Saul. But he never gave up hope that he was going to be king. Like Nelson Mandela, when he was in prison, he envisioned himself as the next president of South Africa.

So we need to speak words to our sons that will build them up. We can heal from broken bones or bruises from falling down. Those negative words from a father might never heal, and they will be daggers in our children's hearts that will stay there for years and maybe the rest of their lives. We might receive healing from the words of our fathers, but sometimes, if they don't, then they will be a reminder to us not to repeat the cycle with our children and grandchildren.

As dads, we need to take inventory of how our dads raised us. We need to see if there are any pitfalls in how our dad raised us so that we do not pass them on to our kids. The crazy thing is that when our kids are young and dependent on us, it is much easier to be a dad. It is when they get older and challenge our authority and our position as a dad that it becomes more challenging than when they are younger. How we navigate our relationship with our sons is crucial during this tough time. We do not want to be on autopilot and assume that our kids are just fine as they age. We must keep the lines of communication open and always be willing to change our approach to guide and direct them into adulthood.

Chapter 4:

Defender of the Weak

Growing up with a sister with Down syndrome and witnessing my father verbally abuse my mother taught me not to appreciate the unfair treatment of others. I developed into a man who stood against anyone who was abused or neglected. I am not afraid of confrontation, and I feel that most people in this world would rather avoid a problem and hope it goes away than confront it. When kids would say rude things to my sister or pick on her, I was not one to ask nicely for them to stop. I would punch them in the face and then tell them they better never talk to my sister again like that.

> Psalms 82:3–4 says, "Give justice to the weak and the fatherless; maintain the rights of the afflicted and the destitute. Rescue the weak and the needy; deliver them from the hands of the wicked."

> Proverbs 31:8–9: Open your mouth for the mute, for the rights of all who are destitute. Open your mouth, judge righteously, defend the rights of the poor and needy.

> Isaiah 1:17: Learn to do good, seek justice, correct oppression: bring justice to the fatherless, plead the widow's cause.

Kids in school can be mean to other kids, especially those with disabilities. I would have to defend my sister on the bus and in our neighborhood. Growing up and constantly protecting my sister and mom has made me sensitive to anyone being mistreated. It has also caused me to become a voice for those who cannot or do not have the courage to speak up on their behalf. I see people always being scared to confront people who mistreat them, but I have never had a problem with facing them. When I moved to

Chicago after returning from the Army, I worked with the homeless and youth involved in gangs.

I was 20 years old, and I had no fear. We used to bus kids to church from the projects. They were dangerous places to live for children. Some kids were 12 to 13 and would be packing heat. For those who don't know what that means, it means having a gun on them. It angered me that the gangbangers made these families live in fear. I would not put up with it. It would remind me of my childhood, and I would be determined that I would stand up to these gang leaders to rescue these kids from their situation of being prisoners to these gang leaders. I was pretty radical for Jesus at the time. I even had scriptures painted all over my car. I would drive my car around Chicago to look for street gang members. Then I would approach them and ask them if they were gangbangers. They would have confused faces, and I would say because I am gang-banging for Jesus. I would also tell them they need to be disciples of Jesus instead of gang members. I worked with two Chicago gangs: the Latin Kings and the Disciples. They were rival gangs. I was eventually able to help 30 kids escape the gangs.

I was deeply longing to make a difference in this world. Looking back on it, I long for people to be proud of me for my accomplishments. The pastor of the church was the one who asked me to come to Chicago to help him with the church. I felt honored that he wanted me to help him with the church. In my twenties, I looked for men in leadership to be father figures for me. I looked for their affirmation and praise, which I did not receive as a child. I had high expectations for these men to be a dad to me, but I was always let down because, at the end of the day, they were not my dad, and it was unfair of me to put them in that position. I was close to the pastor in Chicago, and at times I felt like he treated me like a son because he only had a daughter. The crazy thing is, no matter how badly I wanted a father figure in my life, no man except my real dad could fill that void. I wished for the pastor to fill that void, but he was not looking to be my dad. Those were my expectations, but not his.

When my first wife and I married, she became a church secretary and began to see things that were not handled well in the church, primarily financial, so it began to strain my relationship with him. Additionally, he made a lot of promises to me that he never kept, so I constantly felt let down by a father figure. But during the time that I was there, I was trying to make a difference in their lives for the right reasons. Still, when I look back, I see other motives were because of the needs I didn't get as a child. The need to be appreciated, accepted, and loved.

I remember the pastor telling stories of me working with the street gangs during many of his sermons. It would make me feel so good because I needed the praise in my life. Now that I'm 52, I look back and see my true motives. Don't get me wrong; I still had a desire to help those who were weak or could not fight for themselves, but my motives were not totally pure. It's strange how your childhood experiences influence your future. I have seen that in my life. We will not have the purest motives when we want to accomplish great things.

There are unmet needs in our lives from childhood that cloud those pure intentions. I know that there isn't a perfect family out there. Some are better than others but not perfect, so we will always have a clouded perception while trying to accomplish something. Often, it's not until years later, when we look back, that we realize our true motives. So by not showing any fear of working with street gangs, I look back. It was a way not to show my broken heart from childhood. I also did not have to be vulnerable, and I could look tough. I didn't want people to see what I felt inside. I was less solid and secure than I made everyone think I was. I've known very successful business owners who make millions of dollars tell me how bad their relationship was with their dads. One of my friends has not spoken to his dad in years. It's funny because I really think they push themselves to be so successful in business to maybe find some sense of appreciation from their dads. But most of the time, the dad really doesn't care. And so they keep striving to make more money and do more incredible things. I have tried this with my dad; I would call him and tell him all these great things I'm doing, and he would be indifferent on the phone to me. I would hang up the phone and say to myself, "He will see —I'm going to show him how successful I will become." My dad was a miserable person, and his life did not get better as he got older. He had failed at business, and his health was not good. So instead of trying to turn things around, my dad gave up on his life. He didn't say I would use my failures to help me succeed. He just quit. I said to myself, I will not be like my dad, ever. I'm going to be successful, and he will see.

Psalms 34:18 says, "The Lord is near the broken heart and saves the crushed in spirit."

We have all these grown men running around where their dads have broken their hearts, and that's crushed their spirits. No matter how much they've accomplished, it just doesn't matter—it will not fix the hurt or pain they caused when they were children. I also think many men will try to find comfort in other things to make them not think about the pain. I also believe that some men don't even realize the pain they have in their hearts from their dads. So they will continue to repeat the cycle and go on and be like their dads in their relationships. Whether for the better or worse, our parents shape who we are. Parents significantly influence us, from the foods we eat to how we react to things. So as dads, we have to recognize the pain in our own lives and find healing so that we don't end up doing the same things to our kids.

Chapter Five

Finally Free: So I think

When I reflect on the times I was in my 20s, I think of how cocky and arrogant I was. I thought I had figured my shit out and started what I felt was a new life. I was married with two amazing kids. Life was good. I was telling myself that I was not like my dad. At the time, I was a good husband and a very involved father to my young daughter and son. I was a strong Christian who made a difference in people's lives. What I was doing with my life made me feel that my childhood problems were behind me. However, visiting my parents at my childhood home forced me to relive my past. Seeing my dad was tough, even as a grown, established man. There was still a lot of tension between my mom and dad in the house. My dad would still talk down to my mom.

Growing up, my two older brothers considered me a little brat. It was weird because when I got home and my brothers were there, I would revert back to when I was a kid and start acting like a little brat. I would torment my brothers; it's amazing how words were spoken when you were a little child and how they would define you as an adult. My family's dysfunction would not change just because we were adults and had our own kids. I had to relive my childhood during holidays and special occasions when I went home. I enjoyed going home, but it only took a day or so after being there to realize why I had moved away from my hometown. In the Bible, Jesus was not welcomed in his hometown. He didn't even do miracles in his hometown. Here was a guy doing miracles—raising the dead and healing the sick. When people heard it, they could not believe it was Jesus of Nazareth. Doing these miracles, they were like, "Seriously, this is not Jesus." That's how I felt when I came home from Chicago. Here I was, making a life for myself and so proud of having kids, changing and breaking the cycle of my childhood, and being a great dad. I thought this childhood stuff was behind me, but as soon as I walked in the front door of my childhood home, all these emotions would come flooding back. Oh, how deceived I was, thinking this childhood stuff was behind me. It's funny because I would never have thought I would still be dealing with childhood issues. I believe that in every season of life, you deal with a deeper level of pain from when you were a kid. Or maybe it's when you're done raising kids yourself. You have more time to think about these things. As you get older, you start to reflect more on your childhood. You also begin to dissect the way you raised your kids. It was funny to watch my kids grow up and see the different seasons they went through. I remember when my daughter turned 13. It was a big deal for her to become a teenager. I remember that little girl who used to run into my arms for me to hold her but now will not let me hug her. Like she's doing now because of the coronavirus, but she's in her twenties and married now. But it was hard as a dad at the time. I just had to give her space, thinking she would grow out of it. Which she eventually did. Or when my son entered ninth grade, he stopped playing sports and started skateboarding. In junior high, he played football, basketball, and lacrosse. At the time, I was a high school lacrosse coach, so it was hard when he made that decision. Still, I had to let him make his own decisions. He was trying to find his own identity outside of me.

Now I'm a jock to the core; I play every sport and enjoy watching sports, so when he arrived home wearing skinny jeans, I was not pleased. Thank God he loves playing sports again, like I do now. I had to let him find his identity, which was really hard. I wanted to make him continue playing sports, but I knew that if I pushed him, then I would push him away from me. Seeing your kids try not to be like their parents is amusing, but unfortunately, it is in their DNA, and there is no escaping it. They are going to be like you in many ways. That's why when they become parents and start raising their kids, they will say something to them, and then they will say, I sound just like my mom or dad.

Whenever I went back home, I really thought I was free. I was doing some great things in Chicago. I moved out of the city and started personal training at one of the top health clubs in the country. I was considered one of the health club's top trainers. I also had a successful basketball program where I trained Michael Jordan's kids. Life was good. I am also the proud dad of two great kids. I thought I'd made it in the back of my head. I'm not like my dad; I broke the cycle. How wrong I was. You see, I was just like my dad in many ways. As much as I was in denial that I was just like my dad, there's no denying that I was just like him. I think the trauma or hard times that we go through as kids will never go away. You can find healing in it and use it for positive things in your life. My childhood experience has helped me be a better coach for my players in high school. I can tell just by meeting a kid what kind of parents he has. As parents, we like to control our kids in some way. I mean, you don't want your kids to be robots, but you want to protect them and keep them from the pain you went through as a kid. But sometimes, you can hurt them by not letting them learn from their mistakes. It's hard because I'm still trying to guide my kids in their lives as adults. We want to protect our kids from the pitfalls we once fell into, so we try to steer them away from things, and the harder we push them, the more they will want to go where you are trying to keep them away from. There's a reason why birds kick their young out of the nest. If they didn't, they would never fly, staying in the nest until they were 30.

I wanted my son to succeed in sports and be a great athlete, but that's not what he wanted to do. It's funny because my dad was not an athlete; he liked gardening and woodworking. I am not a gardener. I found my worth in sports, and I still do today. In my twenties, I tried to prove to the world that I was somebody and that I was important. I was also trying to prove to myself that I was not like my dad, and the older I got, the more I realized I was a lot like him. I told myself I would not screw up my kids' lives like my dad did to me because I was a Christian now. I have a new life, and my old life is behind me. I was determined to be the best dad I could be to redeem my messed-up childhood. I was trying so hard to be free that I wasn't dealing with the pain in my life. I was putting up this image that I had all my crap together, a great family, and a great career. I was trying to put up a front so I could feel like I was different from the way my family was.

My new family with my children was not dysfunctional. I thought I was free, but I was still chained to my past and didn't even realize it. Trying to be someone you are not is exhausting. Being the baby of the family is not a bad thing. I am a very spontaneous person, and I love change. Still, I was trying to be the opposite of myself to prove that I was in control of my life and my family, which I was not. So, it is okay to accept the person you have become because of the circumstances in your childhood that have shaped you. There are reasons why you are who you are. At 50, I finally realized I was like my dad. Thank God, because my dad was pretty funny. He made many people laugh. He was the life of the party, and he was not boring. So, I can finally say that I take after my father and accept that now. I am thankful that, even though I am like my dad, I have changed many things about how I parent. I was not perfect, and if I could go back and change a few things, I probably would, but I have no regrets about raising my kids.

Chapter Six:

A Father's Expectations for a Son

I dedicate this chapter to my daughter Tessa Hilton (Tessa Bost) and my son Ty Hilton.

I can remember when I first became a father; the level of excitement was crazy. It was a miracle watching my kids be born. My kids were born at home, so the experience was different from having them in a hospital. My daughter was the first to be born, and she was born on a hide-a-bed couch in our friend's living room. As a father, you always wish to have a boy first, but that didn't happen. So, when my daughter was born, I had her do everything as if she were a boy. She was born during the NBA playoffs, and I had her watch basketball as a newborn. She was going to be in the WNBA, I said to myself. As a father, having a daughter born first was not a bad thing. The bond I had immediately with her was powerful, and it still is today. Now I know you're saying I thought this book was about a father-son relationship, and it is, but I need to lay a foundation for this chapter. Because I believe this chapter deals with the expectations that we as fathers put on our kids, my daughter was the apple of my eye. I could not get enough of her, and I couldn't wait to hold her at the end of the day. I thought to myself that I'm not going to mess this up by being a father like my dad has. I had it all figured out as a dad, and she was only a few weeks old. I had her life all planned out for her, and she didn't even know it. Only God knows the plans for our kids, and we are here to offer guidance and direction and to help facilitate. In previous chapters, I talked about squashing kids' dreams, but what about trying to point them in a direction they do not desire to go? I see this with dads a lot. I had the chance to coach a few kids whose dads were in the NBA, including Michael Jordan's boys, Marcus and Jeffrey, and Horace Grant's son, Horace junior. I also coached Mookie Blaylock's kids. I never knew if their dads' put expectations on their kids to be in the NBA, but the bar was set pretty high for them at the beginning of their lives. Living in the shadows of their father's successful careers in the NBA.

As fathers, we would love for our kids to follow in our footsteps, whether taking over the family business or becoming professional athletes, lawyers, police officers, etc. We must ensure we allow our kids to take the path they think they want. As a dad, it's effortless to be influential in the direction of our kids' lives, but it's their dream, not yours. I was very protective of my daughter. I wanted to make sure she was doted on and that I told her how pretty she was. I call her my peanut. I still call her that today, and she's about to turn 31. I once wanted her to play basketball in the WNBA or college lacrosse at Syracuse, which never ended up happening. She is a successful young lady with extraordinary gifts and talents—too many to write about in this book. My son was born in our mobile home two years after my daughter. I named him Leo Tyrone Hilton, his middle name. Tyrone was named after MUGSY BOGUES in the NBA because he was only 5 ft 3. Mugsy's first name is Tyrone, and he was the shortest player to ever play in the NBA, and he could dunk. My middle name is Terrance, and I always wanted to have my middle name be Tyrone. I figured my son had a chance to make it to the NBA if Mugsy could. Also, I thought how cool it would be for his name to be called out in pregame on a microphone: Leo Tyrone Hilton. I always felt it would be great to see him play in Chicago at the United Center. He was born in a mobile home outside Chicago and is now in the NBA. What a story.

Wake up. You're dreaming, Leo. That's my dream, not my son's. It is incredible how we fantasize about our kids fulfilling dreams of our own that we never achieved ourselves. Now, I'm not saying that if your child is excelling at something and you know that they love it, then it's okay to throw your time and money at it to help them achieve their dreams, but remember, it's their dream, not yours. As the father of a son and a daughter, I treat them significantly differently. I was always harder on my son than my daughter. My wife always knew whom I was talking to on the phone, even by how I answered when they would call. We want our sons to be tough, and I think sometimes we try to push them too hard (as it was for me).

All my daughter had to do was say, "Hey, dad. I love you," and I would ask her how much money she needed. Whereas with my son, it was definitely different. I wanted him to work for things and push himself. As a dad, you want to raise your sons to be able to handle challenging situations. Becoming a father is a ton of responsibility, and there are so many things we need to juggle. It's like having a ton of plates spinning on our hands, and we have to keep them going. I was the only one working at the time. I wasn't making much money, so I had to work a few extra jobs. I was working full-time as a job coach for people with special needs.

At night I would deliver pizzas, and on weekends I would work construction. My kids' mom stayed home, raising two small children and eventually homeschooling them. That was a lot harder than me working three jobs, for sure. I found that out later, when my granddaughter was born, because I got to watch her for a few mornings a week when my daughter-in-law had to go back to work. Between changing diapers and feeding her, you get nothing done.

I never understood that as a young dad. I would come home from work and ask my wife, "What did you do today?" The house was a wreck, and she was still in her pajamas, which was a total disconnect for me. I couldn't understand why she didn't get other things done. I had a lot of expectations of my wife at the time, and as the kids got older, we put expectations on our kids. As a young dad, it's hard to figure out the direction you would like your family to go. It's like grasping at straws; you're just trying to survive and tend to react to problems instead of being proactive. At 23, I thought I was so mature, but now that I'm 52, I look back at my 23-year-old self and realize I was just a kid. If I could go back to that time and talk to myself, I would tell myself as a dad not to major in minor things and not to put huge expectations on my family, especially my kids. I'm not saying you do nothing, but you can set goals for yourself and your family and make them realistic and attainable. Your job as a father will never end. It just changes. Our kids are grown now, but I am still their father. So remember, there is no finish line as a dad. You can say, I can't wait till they're eighteen and move out of the house. Good luck with that. That's a lofty goal—maybe too high of an expectation, buddy. Enjoy where your kids are right now.

Don't wish for them to grow up and move out. Enjoy them now as much as possible in the season you are in. Don't clip your kids' wings either. Put a leash on them. Allow them to dream, spread their wings, and fly. Don't micromanage them and try to do everything for them—I see this a lot as a coach. You have to let your kids struggle and figure things out for themselves. It's hard because you want to clear a path for them to make life easier. You want to give them a plan. I know because I have tried to do that for my kids, especially my son. Showing your kids unconditional love as a father is probably one of the most important things you can do. Also, don't tell them no all the time or say you can't. If they ask you to do something, and it might seem really hard to do, instead of saying no way, say let's see if we can find a way. Also, don't nitpick at your kids. Encourage, encourage, encourage. Build up, build up, build up. Don't discourage; don't be negative; be positive. Believe that you can achieve it if you can dream it.

There are enough negative people in the world. Kids don't need their dads to be one of them. Also, remove the words I can't afford it and I can't. I can't; it's a terrible word. We all use it, so remove it from your vocabulary. My kids grew up thinking money was hard to come by because I always complained about how expensive everything was. I was cheap and never wanted to spend money. In turn, I never had much money because of that mindset. Thank God, I don't think like that anymore.

Encourage your kids to go after what they want and not take no for an answer. I remember one day I came home, and my son at the time was doing parkour, and he was standing on the roof of our house asking me if I thought he could land a backflip off the top. My son is not a considerable daredevil, but he was training in foam pits then, so he had confidence that he could do it. I think most dads would be like, "Son, you better get your butt down from that roof before I kill you." Luckily, his mom was in the house and didn't know he was about to do that. I said to him, "Go ahead. You've got this." He did it first with a few mats on the ground, then got back up there and nailed it without anything on the floor. The excitement and sense of accomplishment on his face was something I will never forget. At the time, he was constantly training in parkour and getting pretty good at it. He had stopped playing sports for his school, which was hard for me. I had wanted him to play in high school and college, but that was my dream. Luckily, I had enough restraint not to push him into sports, but I encouraged him in his parkour. Seeing him not play sports was challenging because he was a good athlete. It's hard to let your kids take their own path in life. My daughter was a three-year starter on her high school lacrosse team, but then she came to me and said she was not going to play her senior year, which, as a high school coach, was tough to chew on, but she wanted to focus on school and other things. She wanted to enjoy her senior year without the pressure of being part of a sports team. It would've been easy for me to put pressure on them to play sports, but in the end, I knew it was best for them to make their own decisions. Tessa ended up taking a year off from college and moving to South Africa, where she got to experience so much working in an orphanage and traveling to other countries. My son ended up doing dual enrollment; he was taking college classes as a senior in high school. And I knew deep down inside that he would never become a professional athlete but would follow his own dreams, and I was okay with it. My kids ended up playing one season of college lacrosse for their club team. As a dad, watching them play in college gave me so much joy.

My daughter is a successful technical writer; she graduated with a communications degree, and my son graduated with a mechanical engineering degree and a minor in aerospace engineering. My son has been working as a mechanical engineer in Indiana now. I'm so proud that they made their own path; the sky is the limit for their success. My daughter is not in the WNBA, and my son is not in the NBA, but I am more proud of them than if they were professional athletes. So in closing, I encourage every dad out there to be excited about what his kids are excited about. Realize the dreams that did not happen for you, and don't try to make them your kids' dreams. Also, enjoy your time while your kids are young and still under your roof, because it goes by fast.

Chapter 7:

I Will Not Be Like My Father to My Kids

I remember saying to my younger self that when I have kids, I will not be like my father was to me. Every kid growing up always says I'm not going to be like my mom or dad in some way—maybe not to the extent of the passion I felt about not being like my dad, but in some small way. When they were little, most boys looked up to their dad and wanted to be like him, but this was not the case for me. When I was 6 or 7, I started building resentment toward my dad. So I didn't have to wait till I got to be a teenager to stop wanting to be like my dad; I never had the desire to follow in my father's footsteps. From a very young age, I tried to run away from home. At 52, I still have the little suitcase where I packed all my clothes in the first grade and told my mom I was leaving. She knew I wouldn't go far, so she let me leave. I wasn't gone long, so I didn't go far before I returned home and unpacked my suitcase. My wife keeps trying to have me get rid of that suitcase, but I can't because every time I look at it, it brings me back to that day. There was no idolizing my dad, that's for sure.

The ages of 1–7 are crucial for children. Their personalities are developing, mirroring those of their parents during this time, so how we lead as examples for them is crucial. So for me, all I had to do was listen to how negative my dad was about everything, complain about how bad the world was, and always be miserable day in and day out. That was not a great role model for me. By the time I was 7, I was already tired of it. I now look at my 7-year-old grandson, Landon, and I love seeing his sense of adventure and excitement for life. He is not one to sit still and watch TV. He reminds me of myself—always on the go. He is the same way when he comes over. We are constantly doing things, from riding bikes to playing basketball or lacrosse to building a fort. I've watched him develop into a person since he was a baby. His behaviors are hardwired now; he is all boy, and I love it.

Now he does get into trouble in school just because he acts like a boy. Boys can't be boys today in school, but that's another subject.

I grew up watching my dad's way of handling conflict in his life, which was not good. He never had a great outlook on life; even in good times, he always had something to complain about, which got hardwired in me as a kid. Now that my kids are grown, I realize I did many of the same things my dad did to raise me. I had a loving relationship with my kids. Still, my communication was much like how my dad communicated. I would say, "Don't do that; you can't do that; we can't afford that." My conversations with my ex-wife were about the same as my dad's conversations with my mom. I had the same conflict resolution skills that my dad had with my mom. I would raise my voice and criticize my ex-wife. Sometimes I would be difficult to deal with, and my ex-wife would submit to not causing additional conflict. Looking back on my failed marriage, I believe that my upbringing and witnessing my parents fight were the main contributing factors. My dad would dominate my mom. My mom would submit.There was no fight at all, just like with my ex-wife. It was not my mom's fault or my ex-wife's fault. It was my fault; I didn't even realize I was doing it until I remarried. My new wife would not put up with my crap. I remember the first apartment we rented together. I was sitting on the couch, and she was getting something in the kitchen. She came out of the kitchen, and I said, "You didn't ask me if I wanted anything." I realized that was a big mistake—insert foot into mouth. She laid into me and said, I don't see you asking me if I want anything while you're in the kitchen. Let's say I got a rude awakening that day. She stood up to me and would not back down. At the beginning of the relationship, we had a lot of knock-down, drag-out fights because she would not allow me to boss her around.

I realized I had to change if I wanted this relationship to work out. I didn't even know I was this way. It was all happening through my subconscious mind. It was a learned behavior I developed watching my dad as a kid. Let's say that my relationship with my second wife was totally different. I have changed a lot, and sometimes I wish I could go back and change things in the past, but I can't. Sometimes my grandson is over, and I will start saying things like, "You can't, don't do that," or "We are not doing that today." My wife will speak up and say, "Stop talking to him like that."

The crazy thing is that I don't even realize that I'm saying it so many times. Our language is imperative to how we communicate with our families. We must build a strong foundation and relationship with our wives and kids. Our children are a lot like us, mainly because they will mirror us as they age and have relationships. My wife has seen my daughter and I argue and she would say, I can't stand when you two argue over something; you both get so loud. My daughter and I are like two big-shot lawyers defending our stance on a subject in a courtroom. My daughter has learned from the best. I could be dead wrong on a topic, but I will defend it to my death—we are both stubborn in that way.

My son is different. He really won't engage in an argument. He will try to defuse it or say, "I'm done. I'm not talking about this anymore." As fathers, we must be role models to our sons in how we treat our wives. I worry about my son because I won't be a great role model when he marries. I've changed a lot in my second marriage; I'm learning to honor my wife and build her up, but I have a long way to go to break those bad habits I learned as a kid from my dad.

Being a husband was totally separate from being a dad. In my first marriage, I was so focused on being a good dad that I didn't focus on my relationship with my kids' mom. The two go hand in hand. Believe me. Your son is going to mirror you. I thought I would be so different from my dad, but when life got tough or I argued with my ex-wife, I turned into my dad and acted just like him. I didn't realize I was hurting my kids until I went through my divorce from my first wife.

I had a personal training studio in my house, and my office was also there. I remember the day I had to call each of my kids into my office to tell them I was moving out and we were getting divorced. It makes me cry to this day thinking about it. That day, I realized I wasn't any better as a father than my father was to me. My failed marriage was now playing a part in messing up my kids' childhood: no more family vacations or dinners. Now the kids have to spend time with mom and dad individually, not together. Holidays were challenging because they had to go to Dad's, and they were no longer spending time together as a family. I thought I was avoiding the pitfalls of my father hurting me as a kid; I thought I was changing and being a better dad, and in some ways, I was. Still, I had created my own pitfalls for my kids' childhood to be negatively affected. It's all connected, but we like to compartmentalize our lives as men. We have work relationships, husband-wife relationships, kids, parents, guardians, siblings, friends, finances, etc. We do an outstanding job of separating everything. Still, it is all connected and affects us in every way. It is so hard to change the behaviors we grew up with.

I've been trying to change myself since I was in my teens, so for for over thirty years and every time I feel like I've made progress, I can fall back into my old ways. One step forward, two steps back—one of the most significant ways that helped me change was hypnotherapy to deal with my subconscious. Dealing with my subconscious changed my behavior patterns. The anger and bitterness I had towards my dad had been hardwired in me since I was a little boy—in the next chapter, I will talk about that in more detail—but the bitterness destroyed everything in my life. I was definitely blaming my dad for all the failures in my life. My failed marriage and business were my fault, not my dad's. I had to stop being a victim and feeling sorry for myself. I created all my problems, not my dad. I had to change myself for my son's sake. I spent a lot of time in front of the mirror talking to myself and yelling at myself to get over my shit—my dad had been dead for a while, and I was still letting him affect me. It was not my dad's fault. It was my fault. Own your own shit. Stop being the victim in your life and take responsibility for your actions.

As I said, everything changed for me when I went through hypnotherapy. My hypnotherapist began to work on my subconscious, and as badly as you want to change things in your life, you can't do it through your conscious mind. You have to do it through your subconscious mind. Hypnotherapy works on the subconscious mind, which is why it is so effective. The hypnotherapist began to speak positive words of affirmation into my subconscious mind. It was so wild because I would fall into a deep sleep, and she would say, Leo, you are falling too deep into hypnosis. My wife would joke and say you're paying her for a good nap. She was kidding and realized it was helping. My conscious mind was off when she told me I was God's creation and deserved good things to happen to me. My conscious mind wasn't saying that was a bunch of crap. It was unbelievable because I didn't feel that good about myself, and after those sessions, good things started to happen to me. I would never have been able to get my pilot's license if I hadn't changed. I would have given up on that after a short period of time, so the hypnotherapy really changed my life. It set me on a course to change my subconscious. I would also listen to YouTube videos of people to help my subconscious: people like Joe Vitali, Jim Rohn, Tony Robbins, Bob Proctor, and Bruce Lipton. I was still broke during this time, and my world had crumbled around me, but my attitude had changed. As a pilot, even your perception of the things around you can affect your attitude, directly impacting how you fly.

How you view the noise of your plane is very important, whether you're climbing in altitude or descending to the ground. So my attitude was changing for the positive, and things were starting to turn around for me. If you allow your nose to drop, you'll lose altitude when flying. If you bring your nose up too much, you will lose airspeed and stall the plane. If you have your nose level and are on the horizon, your aircraft will be in perfect flight. I don't think people realize how they reflect their pain and troubles from childhood on others in their day-to-day lives. As men, we carry so much baggage from our childhood, which weighs us down in life. As a pilot, you must be careful how you load your plane with your luggage. If you have too much luggage, it could cause your plane to crash. So many of us cannot soar and fly to achieve our dreams because of the bags holding us down. In my case, I kept tripping over the baggage in my life. As much as I wanted to, I struggled to be able to change.

Self-growth was impossible until hypnotherapy. The chains from my past broke, freeing me from the torment of my broken childhood. Before hypnotherapy, I had anger and bitterness toward my dad that I would not let go of. I blamed all my problems on my screwed-up childhood and my dad. I was like a rotten piece of fruit. I looked good on the outside but was rotting from the inside out. I think most men try to forget about it and bury the pain that their dad has caused. It doesn't work like that. Your future depends on you getting healed. Your kids and your grandkids will be affected if you don't change. So I thought I was a great dad, but my childhood issues hurt my relationship with my kids. Looking back now, I can see that the pain in my life affected my children. Our decisions today will determine our future tomorrow.

Chapter 8:

Bankrupt and Divorced – Dead and Gone Forever

This chapter is the hardest for me to write of all the chapters in this book. As I mentioned in Chapter 7, hypnotherapy has really changed me. But some of my choices caused me to reap some rotten fruit.

I had just gone through bankruptcy when my second wife and I met. I was 1.4 million dollars in debt, so I had no choice but to file bankruptcy. I had made some terrible real estate deals. Part of it was that the bubble popped and the housing market crashed. At the time, I owned 16 apartments and a brand-new townhome in which no one lived. I trusted some people in business that I should not have counted on. I didn't do any research and just trusted their word that we would make a lot of money on these deals. I had my own fitness business and was doing personal training then.

Remember what I said about the fruit? I was in great shape, but I was rotting inside. The fitness business was making money, but I wanted to make a lot of money, and I thought I could make that happen through real estate. Things might have been okay if the market hadn't crashed, but it did, and I was in a bit of a pickle. So by the time my wife met me, I had just gone through bankruptcy, my dad had died a year before, I was in the middle of a divorce, and my mom was diagnosed with cancer and dying.

Life was so much fun at this time (I'm being sarcastic). I had moved out of my house and rented a room from a guy. I was still trying to keep my fitness business out of the basement of my ex-wife's house. But that was not going so well either because the economy was terrible. Looking back, I can't believe my new wife wanted to be with me. I love her so much because she loved me even at the lowest point in my life. Most women would have run the other way, but not her—she stood by me. Before I met my wife, I was at a shallow point in my life before I went through hypnotherapy. There were times when

I was ready to end it all. There were times I was driving down the road and thought I could bury my car in a tree and end it all, but I thought of my kids and how I would mess them up. It makes me cry to this day to think about that time. I think people become so desperate that they don't see any other way out. My kids definitely kept me fighting in life and not giving up.

My cousin took his life when he was 16. My aunt and uncle found him hanging in their basement. When he was ten, a neighborhood boy who was older than him molested him. He had gotten into drugs because the pain was so bad, and he couldn't take it anymore. It devastated my aunt and uncle. My uncle was never the same again. My uncle died because he just let his health go. My aunt has always lived with the pain of losing her only son.

Seeing that made me think about how it would affect my kids if I did something like that. Suicide is a permanent solution to a temporary problem. Hardships, failures, and struggles are not always bad things. It has taught me a lot of lessons in life. I thank God for everything he has brought me through. I would not be the husband, father, or grandfather I am today if I had not gone through the hard times.

Sometimes all we can do is hold on and not give up. We have seasons in life, and we are not guaranteed that they will go as planned. You might be reading this book when your world collapses around you and you feel like giving up, but you have to keep fighting because your family needs you. Because of my hardships, I have been able to help my kids navigate through their young adult lives. Your season will change, and you will come out of this time stronger than before. When you have gone through the deepest and darkest valley in your life and ascended to the highest mountaintop, you will appreciate it much more. God has restored everything I lost in my life, and now I know that if I lose everything again, with God's help, I can get it back. You have to be honest with yourself, not make excuses for yourself, take full responsibility, and not act like it's someone else's fault—your dad, your wife, your boss, your kids, your dog. In our world today, people like to blame everyone for their problems instead of taking responsibility for their actions. When I was younger, I did a lot of stupid things. Now that I'm older, I don't do as many stupid things. It helps to have a strong wife who tells me I'm about to do something stupid. Sometimes I don't listen to my wife; she has to remind me that she told me not to do that. I wouldn't be where I am today without my wife. She has always been the voice of reason for me.

About a year ago, I wanted to buy ten acres in Tennessee, and she kept telling me this was not a good time for us. I was busy coaching lacrosse and had little time in my schedule. But I was determined to make it work. I even had my daughter and her husband interested in buying a ten-acre lot also. I even put $5,000 deposit on the property. The good thing was that I had thirty days to back out and not lose that deposit.
We visited the property several times, and my wife was uncomfortable with it. After a couple of weeks, I decided to back out of the deal. Looking back on that, I see how that would not have been a good decision. My wife helped me because I would've pulled the trigger on that. Your choices today will affect your decisions tomorrow. I didn't get that in my 20s and 30s, but in my 50s, I'm slightly getting it.

In general, it's hard for people to make decisions. We are taught in school not to make mistakes or fail. But the only way to grow in life is to make mistakes, learn from them, and not make them again. Being indecisive is a disease of success, so many people are afraid to take a risk in life. We live in a world where we are all about safety. I can't stand people who tell me to be safe or drive safely. I tell them, "No, I'm going to be reckless and drive crazy." Just ask my wife. My kids bought me a shirt for Father's Day that said, "Risk takers or reckless people might not live long lives, but the cautious don't live at all. This society that we live in today is really about living life in fear. People today listen to the news and cancel everything because there's a chance of a storm. It's not even happened, but they fear the worst: our education system in this country has failed our kids. Because they teach them to be fearful, not to make mistakes, and not to fail, most kids these days can't come out of college and create their own opportunities to make money. They have to work for a company. We don't teach kids in school to go after their dreams. We teach them how not to fail and get good grades. We tell them that failing is a bad thing.

Life is an adventure. It's not meant to be boring. It's okay if the decisions you make are not good ones. The Bible says all things work together for good for those who love God. I've made some horrible decisions, and it definitely hurts after realizing it was a bad decision. Still, the mistakes you make will help you in the future if you don't repeat them. Fear is the opposite of faith. I meet people with so much fear in life that they fear their own shadow. I own a motorcycle, and when I tell people that I ride, they say they are dangerous, and I say, "Yeah, but they are fun to ride." Dangerous things in life are fun to do.

I petted a crocodile in Africa. Now that was fun. He was in a fenced area, and his snout was against the fence. I was not supposed to be in this area at the zoo in Uganda, but I was. I told my driver to take a picture of me petting this crocodile; he thought I was crazy, so I went over, put my hand through the fence, onto his snout, and patted him. I asked my driver, "Did you get the picture?" He said no. I had to show him how to retake the picture, and then I reached into the fence and asked him if he got the picture. He said no again, so I had to show him how to operate the camera again. I'm like, "Great, I petted him twice and still have my hand attached." So I went over there a third time and petted him. At the same time, my driver snapped the picture, the crocodile tried to bite me and I pulled my hand away quickly. Great now I get a picture of me pulling my hand away, but I still have my hand attached.

It was funny because we walked by the lion's cage. He looked at me and said, "Are you gonna jump in there?" I said, "I'm not that stupid." Fear is a significant factor when we have to make a big decision in life. Let's say you want to quit your job to start a company, but you say, "What if it doesn't work out? And then I lost my job." You have to ask yourself, "What happens if I succeed and become really wealthy?" When my wife and I pick up a cleaning account, it could add 4-5k a year to our income. A regular job is not going to give you a raise like that. I watched my dad fail at business, and he almost lost our house. And instead of taking advantage of his learning experience, he just gave up. I watched him lose interest in life, and he was miserable. My mom worked hard, not making much money per hour, and he just let his health go. When I saw that he had given up, I told myself, "If this happens to me, I will not give up as he did." While going through bankruptcy, I kept thinking about my dad and how he chose not to fight and get up when knocked down. I had to keep saying to myself, "I have to not give up for my kids' sake." In three years, I lost both my parents, went through bankruptcy, and got divorced. It was brutal, but I just kept fighting. Now, when I look back at that time, it really helped me grow as a person. Les Brown said if you get knocked on your back and can still look up and see the sky, then you still have hope and can still get up. I know now that if I lose everything again, it will be okay. Just like Paul, who lost everything, God restored everything. He even gained double what he had before.

Like I said before, God has restored my life and blessed me beyond what I could have imagined. Although both of my parents are gone, that is tough because I would've loved for them to see me get back up and fight. I would love it if my parents saw me get my pilot's license and take them flying. Life is a blessing, and every day that you are above ground is a gift. We must take advantage of the time because it goes fast.

The Bible says life is like a vapor, here today and gone tomorrow. We cannot blame our parents for our failures. We have to own our own mistakes and learn from them. Our pasts are our pasts. It does not determine our future. Leave the past in the past, look forward to the future, and believe you have great things in store. God is bigger than all of our problems. He can turn your problems into miracles. He has for me. Learn to be thankful instead of complaining and being miserable. Learn to appreciate the little things in life; don't be bitter about past failures. Use them to motivate you to do anything if you make it through the hard times. You have the power to create the world you live in.

Embracing the future, I have realized that every struggle has its purpose. The journey is not about avoiding failure but about learning to rise stronger each time we fall. It's about nurturing resilience, which my experiences have taught me well.

Through the challenges I faced—bankruptcy, loss, and divorce—I discovered the depths of my own strength. I learned that it's okay to lean on others when needed, that vulnerability can be a strength, and that true courage lies in facing our fears head-on.

As I navigate this journey of life, I am committed to being a better husband, father, and grandfather. I strive to instill in my children the values of perseverance, responsibility, and faith. I want them to know that life may throw curveballs, but they have the power to overcome any obstacle with hard work and determination.

Every day is an opportunity to build a better future, not just for ourselves but for those we love. The legacy we leave behind is shaped not only by our successes but also by how we rise after we fall. As I reflect on my life, I know that my past does not define me; rather, it is a series of lessons that have prepared me for the challenges ahead.

Now, as I stand on the brink of new opportunities, I carry with me the wisdom of my experiences. I embrace the journey, recognizing that every step forward is a chance to grow and thrive. With faith as my guide, I look toward the future with hope, knowing that I can create a life filled with purpose, love, and resilience.

Chapter 9:

Filling in the Gap

Today, as I write this book, we are still in the middle of the coronavirus and experiencing riots across America because of racial issues. I see people living in fear of the virus. They are scared to leave the house—people wearing masks and trying to distance themselves socially. People have become scared and allowed fear to control their lives. That is no way to live.

This chapter is not about today's events but about the importance of our parents in our lives. I know this book is about a fatherless son and the importance of a father, which is true. Many problems plaguing the African American community stem from the lack of fathers in the home. In the 1950s, in America, there were 5 percent. Today, it's 40 percent across the board. But among African-American boys, 70 percent grew up without a father in the home. This is a huge problem for these boys as they grow into men. A high percentage of them don't finish high school and end up committing crimes, on drugs, or in prison.

The breakdown of the family unit in America is a huge problem. For many of these kids who grew up without a father in the home, their mother has to fill in the gap. I've heard some amazing stories of moms doing amazing things for their kids who don't have dads. They must work full-time, come home, cook, clean, and help their kids with homework. They must nurture and be strong disciplinary figures in their kids' lives. The children blessed enough to have a mother with this kind of strength have a chance to succeed in life. But only a small percentage of moms can do this; it is a miracle when they do it. I'm thankful my mom was able to nurture me and show me love. I think it saved me from going down the wrong road. She worked hard daily to cook, clean, and help us with whatever we needed. She also worked full-time, had a daughter with Down syndrome, and needed special attention. My mom worked tirelessly to take care of her kids. So she definitely made up for some areas where my dad failed. It is a must, if the dad is not around or if he is in the home and emotionally detached, for the mom to step up and fill that gap, as hard as it may be.

Both parents would be ideal, and if you're blessed enough to have a father and mother there for you, you are truly blessed and should not take it for granted. I longed for that. I would be jealous when I saw kids with their moms and dads who had a vested interest in their lives. Unfortunately, we do not live in a perfect world, so we must make the best of what we have to work with. If you are a single mom raising your kids, you can fill that gap where the father is not. But it would be best to have boundaries and discipline for your children, especially your boys. Or otherwise, they will run amuck. Also, getting your kids involved in sports will help, especially if they have good coaches who can support them and help bring discipline and structure to them. When on a team, you must learn to work with kids you might not like or are different. Also, sports help kids learn about defeat, getting knocked down, getting back up, and not quitting. Coaches have played a huge part in my life to help provide support and be that male figure for me to look up to since my dad did not do that. I am so passionate about coaching because I provide hope to these kids, who sometimes don't have any. As I've said in previous chapters, sports were a huge refuge for me. While I was growing up. Most men don't realize their importance in their kids' lives. Coaches and leaders in the community can play a huge role in developing boys who do not have a father.

I have a story about my high school basketball coach in this chapter. His name is Nick Alvaro. He was a crazy basketball coach, but the kind of guy that, as a player, you wanted to be like. He was a tough coach but a fair coach. When he got mad, he would make us run and utter several four-letter words at us. He was also good at playing basketball; he would take these crazy shots, and they would go in. I learned a lot of moves from him that, at age 52, I still use today. He also had a lot of knowledge to offer about basketball. He could make kids play as a team, which is hard for many wild teenagers to get on the same page. I look forward to going to practice and our games. At the time, I didn't realize he was providing emotional support for me, but as I look back, he did.

There's this term called leaning in. You focus a little more on certain kids on your team than others because you know they need more of your attention than the other kids because you know they have problems at home or need your support a little more than other kids. It's like having your own children. One child might need you more than the other at the time, so you show them more attention. It is so funny because, until I started writing this chapter, I didn't realize that this coach, Nick Alvaro, had this much impact on my life in high school.

He coached me for two seasons in the 9th and 11th grades. God puts people in your life to help you along the way, and you don't even realize it. My coach would cuss like a sailor and he was rough around the edges, but he truly cared about his players.

So several years later, I ended up seeing my coach again. I was home for Christmas to spend time with my mom. I was living in Atlanta, where I still live now. My mom always wanted us to go to church with her on Christmas if we were home. At the time, my mom was not feeling well and was not eating much, but she went to church anyways. When we arrived at church, I looked up to see my old basketball coach leading the service. I was shocked. Here was this guy who used to cuss me out, and he was different and had changed. He had become a full-time deacon for the Catholic Church; the same way he held my attention in the locker room before a game, he could also do it in the church. He is a gifted communicator. It was a nice service, and after the service, we had time to catch up and talk about the good old days.

After Christmas, probably in January, we discovered my mom was diagnosed with cancer, and the outlook was not good. After a few months, her health was declining, so I decided to take a few months off to move up there and be her caretaker. About a day or two before I was about to leave, I got a call from my brother that she was admitted to the hospital, was in intensive care, and might not live long. I scrambled, got in my car, and drove about 100 miles per hour from Atlanta to Syracuse. It usually takes 17 hours, and I think it made it in 13 or 14 hours that night. The funny thing is that my high school coach was now my mom's pastor while she was dying in the hospital. I called him and told him my mom was not doing well, and he said he would be up at the hospital immediately. My mom wasn't supposed to live longer than a day, but she lived for a week after I arrived. And she could be awake, and we got to spend a lot of time together. My coach was up at the hospital several times that week. He was there to comfort her during this time.

Who would've thought that my high school basketball coach played such a huge role in our lives? My coach was there when my mom passed. He was there to pray with us and to comfort us. He ended up doing the funeral and burying my mom.

This is another reason why being a coach is not something I do just to do it. It is a calling for me. I used to be a minister and a youth pastor, but I've found that coaching is my true calling in life. I don't get paid much money, but I love doing it. I love being around teenagers. In some ways, it keeps me young at heart and gives me purpose in life.

But you don't have to be a coach to be a father to the fatherless. You can be a boy scout leader, a teacher, a pastor, or a youth pastor. Teachers can play a huge role in kids' lives. There is a huge need today for men to step up and make a difference in boys' lives who don't have fathers. You might be the cool dad in the neighborhood for kids who don't have a dad. Don't shrug it off and think you're not making a difference. You could play a huge role in these kids' lives who don't have dads to turn to.

Growing up, I had a lot of bitterness towards my dad because I felt like he could care less about me. I wish I could have had the bond that my son and I have. But as I write this book, I finally realize that God puts coaches and teachers in my life to be a father to me where my father couldn't be. It makes me realize I am the man I am today because of these men, who were father figures to the fatherless son. Who knows what would have happened to me if it wasn't for them? I could be in jail, hooked on drugs, or homeless. I can honestly look back at my childhood and say, "You know, it was hard, but having these coaches in my life was powerful to push me to be a better person." It gives me more resolve to push myself to be a better coach and mentor to kids who don't have a father. It's compelling to realize that these men were put in your life to help you along your journey. My dad had a lot of issues in his life that he never dealt with. I am not sure if he had too much pain from his childhood. He just buried it and never wanted to talk about it, but I can honestly say today that I forgive the father he was not to me.

Sins get passed down from generation to generation unless you are willing to confess your mistakes. I have not been the perfect father to my kids, but I sure do own up to my mistakes. We all can make changes in our lives and not allow our parents' mistakes to be our mistakes. That is why I am always trying to help my kids not make the same mistakes I've made in relationships, financial situations, and many other pitfalls I have fallen into to help them stay clear of them.

Chapter 10:

Importance of Family

October 12th, 2020, I can remember the day like it was yesterday. My oldest brother had just visited us in Atlanta a few weeks prior. He was here for about 5 days, and we had a great time going out on our boat and just hanging out with each other. Growing up, my brother Ed was quite different than I was. I was a jock playing multiple sports and he was into working on cars, building stuff, hunting, and fishing. Stuff that takes patience.

It was a Monday, and most of my Lacrosse players did not have school that day. I was out on the field for most of the day coaching lessons. I finished my lessons, got in my truck and I saw my brother had called me. I figured he was just calling to say hello. I called my brother back and to my surprise my nephew answered the phone crying, while saying "Dad is dead."

You hear stories of friends that get calls like that, but that had never happened to me before that day. It was devastating news. I responded, "David what happened?" My nephew said he had a massive heart attack while my nephew and his father were in the woods cutting firewood. The ambulance could not get back to him and my nephew had to pull my brother off his tractor and try to give him CPR. Paramedics finally got to him and rushed him to the hospital, but it was too late. My brother was pronounced dead at 57 at the hospital.

I thought "I will never be able to go snowmobiling with him or snow skiing or just hanging out drinking a beer." I could not believe my brother was dead at such a young age. He had been very healthy and had no major health problems. I felt very vulnerable after this tragic day in my life.

Before my brother passed away, I had always had this mentality that I was indestructible. I thought nothing could hurt me, and I would live forever. Well, that day changed everything. I started to feel like if he died and he was skinnier than me, then something could happen to me. The Bible says that life is like a vapor here today, gone tomorrow. It's very true that time goes by so fast, and I feel at times we take our family for granted. We think they will always be with us and never die.

We get so busy with our careers and our social circles that we neglect spending time with the most important people in our lives, which is our family. When we are finally with our family, we can be distracted by our phones and technology. In some ways technology has helped us, but I feel it has hurt us way more than helping our lives.

My wife and I talk about it all the time. We agree that at the end of the day it is our family that is going to be there for us in times of difficulties. My wife and I have a great social network. We have a ton of friends and acquaintances. However, when you really get down to the nitty gritty, it's your family that has your back. I have never heard anyone, who is lying on their death bed, say I wish I worked more or hung out with my friends more. It is always I wish I would have spent more time with my kids or my family.

I would like to encourage parents to spend more time with your kids, and to get off your phone. In fact, just turn it off so they have your undivided attention. I see parents at the park while their kids are on the playground playing. Instead of paying attention to their kids, they are sitting on a bench on their stupid phones. They are more concerned about what's going on with Facebook instead of engaging with their children. The same is true when kids become adults. They get busy with their young careers and social life and they don't bother spending time with their aging parents. Family comes first, and it should be the main priority. It is for my wife and me. We love hanging out with our friends. We have a lot of really good friends that we love dearly, but our family comes first. It is a priority over our friends and even over making money in our business.

As I look back at raising my kids as a young dad, there are things that I wouldn't change and then some things that I would change. One thing that I would change is how I communicate to my kids. I see a lot of parents saying to their kids "you're stupid" or "you can never do anything right" or "you will never amount to anything." My dad said that crap to me, and it took years to get those words out of my head. At times I can still hear him saying that negative crap.

Now I didn't say that to my kids, but I would always be worried about finances. I would say "money doesn't grow on trees" or "we can't afford that." Now with my grandson I tell him that I have a money tree in the backyard. I want him to feel that money does grow on trees so that he believes that all his needs and even his wants will be met. I changed my poverty mind to a prosperity mind. My grandson keeps asking my wife where my money tree is. I feel that the words that we speak and our actions towards our kids will have a lifetime effect on them. It will either be for the positive or the negative, and it's up to us to shape their future.

Our children observe our lives closely, modeling their behaviors after ours—even down to the foods we eat and our attitudes toward life's challenges. If we eat healthy foods, our kids will likely want to eat healthy foods. If we maintain a positive outlook, they are more likely to do the same. Conversely, if we consume unhealthy foods or complain about every problem like my dad did, these behaviors can become ingrained in their subconscious. I am constantly working to change my bad habits from childhood. My wife often asks me to stop complaining about things, and sometimes I do it without realizing. Fortunately, I have changed my poor eating habits.

As a kid, I loved pizza and ate it almost every night because my parents gave up trying to make me eat what they cooked. When I was in my twenties, raising my kids, I didn't realize how my actions and demeanor could affect them. My son shared my love for pizza. When he was diagnosed with asthma and suffered from severe acne, we had him tested for food allergies. We discovered he was allergic to gluten and dairy. That meant no more pizza and many other foods we enjoyed together.

I made many mistakes in my younger years as a dad, but the most important thing is to love your kids unconditionally and not provoke them. The Bible says that love covers a multitude of sins, and I believe that includes mistakes. When we confess our mistakes to our children and apologize, they grow up to be levelheaded adults.

It's amusing to see my son now; he's a lot like me. He loves wearing athletic gear except at work, where he's an engineer. He is a levelheaded young man, not cocky like I was in my twenties. He avoids the mistakes I made at his age, probably because I shared my pitfalls with him. Opening up and being vulnerable with your sons about your past mistakes makes a huge difference.

Being a father is a great gift from God, often taken for granted until our kids leave the nest. It is truly a blessing to have children, even though they can test our patience and make us angry. However, if we raise them right, they will be there for us in our old age.

The Bible says you are the priest of your home, providing safety, protection, and direction for your family. In my youth, I didn't grasp how my decisions would shape my family's future, for better or worse.

In today's world, many things can distract us from focusing on our families as dads. I believe the biggest issue is not work or social activities, but technology. People spend their days buried in their phones, trying to keep up with social media. Families at dinner often sit silently on their phones instead of talking to each other. This loss of personal interaction and social connection leads to depression because people don't engage with their friends and family.

When parents come home from work, they should put away their phones and spend time with their family. I know it's hard—I struggle with it too—but my wife and I try not to use our phones during dinner or when we have friends and family over.

Social media platforms like Facebook, Twitter (now X), Snapchat, and TikTok can drain our energy. We do benefit from technology. For example, my wife and I were able to call 911 immediately after witnessing a motorcycle slam into a car and go flying through the air onto a sidewalk. In times like those your phone can be a life saver to someone in trouble. Thank God he survived the crash.

Fathers, remember that life is a gift, and your sons are a blessing. Invest in them, mentor them, and be present. Don't pass on your childhood baggage to them. Break the cycle; it's tough, but you can do it. Recognize your mistakes and apologize if you hurt your son. Don't be afraid to say you are wrong in front of your sons. I have and it deepens your relationship with them. Being vulnerable and admitting when you're wrong strengthens your relationship and encourages your sons to share their struggles with you.

Don't be overly serious; be silly with your children and spend one-on-one time with them. When my son came home from Indiana, his company allowed him to work remotely. Even though he's 26 and it was the middle of a busy lacrosse season, I prioritized spending time with him. We had planned to meet up with my daughter on Saturday and spend the day together. Well at the last minute we got added a few games on Saturday to our schedule and I told the other coaches that I can't make it because I am spending time with my kids. Now I wanted to be there with my team but my kids are more important. We ended up grabbing coffee and playing tennis together.

I love coaching and rarely miss practices or games, but family comes first. There's a song by Holly Dunn called "Daddy's Hands" that beautifully describes a father's love and strength. "I remember Daddy's hands, folded silently in prayer and reaching out to hold me when I had a nightmare. You could read quite a story in the calluses and lines". I hope my kids will remember me with similar fondness and love, despite my faults.

I hope that the one day when I am gone that my kids can look back and have great memories of my life as their dad. I have done a lot of crazy things so I know that they will be telling stories to their kids and grandkids at how much fun they had being raised by me. Unlike my dad when he passed away it took me years to forgive him and to receive healing from the wounds that he created from my childhood. It's a journey in life to receive healing and to forgive my dad for the trauma that is in my life. But if we face it head on we can overcome and actually look back with love and forgiveness for my dad and to actually say to my dad that is no longer with us on earth that I love you and thank you for the things that you tried to do for me.

Poem by Allen Shaw

"Dad. I am often told I am just like you. I am honored beyond measure if that is true. You were the best example of what a man should be. I am overwhelmed that someone would say that of me. I never told you enough how proud I am to be called your son. Now that you are gone, I want to tell everyone that you gave me more than a name. Someday I hope your son says the same".

Now I am a lot like my dad and that is for sure but I wish I could relate with this poem for my dad, but I can't and I am ok with that. I hope that our sons will feel that way about us when we are gone.

When I think of moments when my kids tell me they are proud of me, it brings tears to my eyes because I missed that growing up. After I received my pilot's license, my son and daughter expressed their pride, which meant the world to me. If it means so much to us as parents when our kids praise us, imagine how important it is to tell them how proud we are of their achievements. My wife and I are constantly amazed by our talented children and their accomplishments. We have some very talented kids and we are blown away at their achievements. Our son Kelly builds furniture and the things he creates blows us away. Our daughter was a technical writer and musician and artist and it's amazing to see things she creates. Our son Ty is an engineer, and it blows me away how smart he is. Our son Taylor just finished a very difficult course on computer coding and when he shows us stuff he is working on my wife and I look at each other like how does he do that.

In closing this chapter, I want to mention our favorite country singer, Kane Brown. He grew up without a dad and faced a rough childhood, which he often reflects on in his powerful lyrics. His song "I Grew Up Without a Dad" resonates with me, as it echoes my own experiences.

The song's message is about being the best dad you can be despite the past. You can choose to be a victim of your childhood or rise above it. Your future depends on your mindset. Don't repeat your father's mistakes; become a great dad for your sons. Future generations depend on it.

You can choose to be victorious or you can stay a victim of your childhood. Your future depends on what your mindset will be. Don't repeat your father's mistakes; instead, change and become a great dad for your sons. Our future generations depend on it. Kane Brown is a changed man because of not having a father in his life and having a rough childhood, but he is determined to be the best dad that he can be, and I pray to God that he is.

If you're reading this book and you think to yourself that your dad is not a bad dad and has been amazing to you and supported you throughout your childhood, then cherish that and tell him how much he means to you. Spend time with your dad because life is short and you never know when our loved ones will be gone from us. My nephew and nieces are without a dad. They never thought that my brother would die so young.

Michael Jordan's dad was his best friend, and his life was cut short because he was murdered. His dad was there for him in all of his struggles and successes. Brett Favre's dad was killed in a car wreck, and he was really close to him as well. I am sure they both would give up all of their fame and fortune to be able to spend more time with their dads.

Family should be our number one priority in our lives. Do not take your wife, kids, parents, siblings, and grandparents for granted. It is so easy to do in our busy lives. Writing this book makes me want to shout from the rooftops for people to wake up and realize the importance of family. We can never have enough time with our families. People are shocked when a loved one dies suddenly. The first thing they say is, "I wish I had spent more time with them." Or, "If I had known they were going to pass away, I would have spent more time with them."

I have almost died several times in my lifetime. I have had angels that have protected me many times.

The other day, I was heading home from practice on my motorcycle, doing about 60 miles per hour. I looked over to my right and saw a friend that I knew. I tried to beep my horn to get her attention, and when I looked back to my left, I was headed straight for the curb and the median where there were trees. I tried to turn to avoid going into the median and hitting a tree. I rode the top of the curb sideways for about a few football fields. I never lost control, which was crazy and a miracle. My wife and my granddaughter were waiting for me to come home. I thought, "What if I had crashed and didn't make it home?" I thanked God for protecting me. Life is precious, and so are our loved ones, so take the time to spend with your family.

Chapter 11

Creating memories that last a lifetime

Receiving a call that someone suddenly passed away in your family can be the worst thing that can ever happen to you, like when I received the news that my brother suddenly passed away in October of 2020. Fast forward to the month of March in 2021, my wife had been dealing with a swollen tonsil. She got an appointment with an ENT for them to see what was going on with her tonsil. My wife called me crying to say that they think she has cancer. She was crying on the phone, and I wasn't able to be there to comfort her.

To say it was a shock would be an understatement. My 46-year-old wife, who is healthy and a very strong woman, was diagnosed with cancer. After losing my brother just a few months before, I thought I could not afford to lose my wife. I knew that it was going to change every aspect of our lives. My wife is such a rock for our family and makes a lot of sacrifices. The hard part was telling our kids and the rest of our family that she had cancer. The ENT referred us to a head and neck specialist. When we went to the appointment, they put a scope down her nose so they could see what was wrong. There was a tumor on her tonsil that had caused her mouth to not be able to open very much. They wanted to do radiation and chemo to treat her.

When we left the appointment, we sat in the car and talked about our options. We decided that it would be better for us to treat it naturally and not go the medical route. We decided to use the Gerson therapy, which is very strict in what you can eat. You have to radically change your diet: no sugar or salt or any processed foods. She had to juice thirteen times a day with various fruits and vegetables; it was a full-time job. My wife basically healed herself through her dedication and discipline. I admired her dedication, and I thought if I ever received a diagnosis like this, that number one, Would I have the courage she did, and number two, Would I have the discipline. I don't think that I would like she did. Within six months, the tumor had shrunk and was pretty much gone.

It definitely made me realize how much I love my wife and all of the memories that we have created in just a decade of marriage. I took for granted our relationship until I realized that I might lose her. It's very easy to take for granted our loved ones and think they will always be there. We have to cherish our times together with our family and invest in our relationships and continue to make new memories.

Kane Brown sings a song about his wife called "Worship You." He is very wise for his age and understands the importance of his marriage to his wife. He talks about if she were a religion, he might have to worship her, meaning his love for her is so deep that he could worship her the same way that we worship God.

I remember when I first met my wife and how excited I would get when I knew we were going to see each other. How I didn't want to get off the phone with her or have her leave my house to go home. The butterflies and anticipation of seeing her again. It's very easy after being married for a while and having a family to stop investing in the relationship, and I felt like I was doing that until she got diagnosed with cancer and it woke me up to say, man, I really love my wife.

Now, I know you're saying, Leo, hold up, I thought we were talking about a father and son relationship. Well, we are. Kane Brown learned that in order to be a good dad, you have to be a good husband and a role model in how a man should treat his wife.

When your son meets that special someone, he is going to remember all of those times and know how to love and treat a lady. You are his example, and he will model it, good or bad. He will treat his wife the same way you treat your wife.

I think that was my mistake: I thought that all I had to do was be a great dad to my kids, and I didn't focus on being a great husband. My wife and I have now been married for 12 years. Looking back on those 12 years of marriage, it wasn't until my wife was diagnosed with cancer that it finally woke me up to realize that I needed to be a better husband to my wife.

I feel I was trying my best, but I was still being selfish and putting myself first and keeping score in our relationship. I would say to myself, if I do something nice for her, I better get something in return. If I buy her something for Christmas or her birthday and spend a certain amount, then on my birthday or for Christmas she should spend the same or more on me. Keeping score should not be in your marriage. As a husband, you should be willing to sacrifice everything and lay down your life for your wife. In our relationships with our wives, I think our perception of how invested we are is distorted. You might feel you give a lot, but that doesn't mean your wife feels the same way. I can say that my perception was distorted.

I can honestly say that when my wife was diagnosed with cancer, it opened my eyes and made me realize that I needed to do more. I thought I was doing more by trying to juice for her and buying her flowers, but for her, she felt like I could do more and that I was still self-absorbed. Looking back, she was right. Her world was rocked, and she had to change everything from her diet to her lifestyle, but for me, my life went on and nothing changed.

I needed to be her rock during this time, and to a certain degree, I was, but I definitely fell short of being more of a support to her and trying to lighten her load during this difficult time. I share this with you because my son has seen me not being a good husband to his mom. Then he got to witness me struggling to be a good husband to his stepmom. It will show up in their relationship with their girlfriend or wife if we don't model how to be a great husband.

(Memories)

I remember the first time we went to see my son in Indiana after he had moved away to take his first job out of college. We went out to dinner that night and had some drinks. The night started off really nice because it was a cool summer night, and we were playing corn hole and just enjoying each other's company. Then, for some reason, I started to be a smart ass to my wife and not treating her well. I had been drinking a lot. We decided to leave and go back to my son's apartment. Me being stupid made my son stop at the liquor store to buy some more wine. My son begrudgingly stopped for me.

When we got back to his apartment, we decided to play some cards, and I think I was losing because I hate to lose. I started back being a smart ass to my wife. Things got really heated, and we went at each other, and my son had to step in and separate us. I thought for sure I am done with this marriage, and my son got to witness all of the nasty things that I said to my wife. My son has seen us argue with each other but nothing to this magnitude. It was downright embarrassing for my son to have to see this but also to have to step in the middle of us so we wouldn't kill each other.

After that fight, I said I will never let that happen again. I apologized to my son, and since that day, I have tried to be a better role model to him. We can use our past failures to work on our character flaws and make changes to our bad behavior patterns. Behavior patterns are tough to break, but if we work hard and try to change the way we think and act, we can progress and not continue with the same patterns. What's the method of insanity? To do the same thing and expect a different outcome.

To close this chapter, I would like to talk about some of my great memories as a kid. Now, even though my childhood was challenging and sometimes downright unbearable, I can still look back at the great times I had and the times my dad tried hard and made sacrifices for us.

Every year, we would go to Cape Cod and stay in a cottage on the beach for two weeks, and those two weeks were always the best two weeks of my year. My dad had his own business, so he didn't get paid when he didn't work, so it was a sacrifice for him to take us on vacation. Even though it was for him as much as it was for us, he was always way more relaxed (maybe because he drank beer the majority of the time) than when he was at home. Plus, we were always out on the beach and doing our own thing in the cottage. But it was an amazing time, and I have great memories.

My dad also had a pool put in the backyard for us, and every winter, he would make an ice skating rink in the backyard so we could play hockey. We also would have neighborhood parties at our house that were a blast. So, in a way, my dad showed us love in different ways that I really didn't figure out till I was an adult.

My kids went through a tough time with their mom and dad going through a divorce, but it makes me light up when they talk about their memories of the trips we took as a family and all of the good times we had. Those memories will last them long after I am gone.

I have done some crazy things with my kids to create some great memories for them. I went skydiving with my daughter on her 18th birthday, where my chute almost didn't open. That was fun. We rented a pontoon boat in Perdido Bay in Florida where I saw a school of dolphins, and I jumped in the water in the middle of them. My daughter was yelling at me because I scared them all away. I told her I wanted to swim with dolphins. That is a memory that my son and daughter will never forget.

Be spontaneous with your kids; don't be a stick in the mud. Boys are meant to be adventurous and take risks; don't be fearful with your kids. Don't use words like "be safe" or "be careful; you could hurt yourself." Don't go out in the rain; you could catch a cold. It's too cold outside; you could freeze to death. The cold is actually good for you; that's why athletes use ice baths for recovery. We try to keep our kids in a bubble so they won't get hurt, but that's not helping them; it's hurting them. Teach them to not be scared and to be fearless, not fearful.

In today's world, the media does a great job of preaching fear into people's lives. Through the coronavirus, I have watched people live in such fear that they isolated themselves from their family and friends. I watched parents put masks on their kids to make them afraid of something that had a very small chance of affecting them, not to mention that masks don't protect you anyways. If you listen to the news, the world is such a scary place to live in when in fact it's probably safer than 50 years ago because nobody can do anything without it being caught on a camera. There are more crimes solved because of so many cameras that we have today. Also, the technology that we have to predict the weather helps us with bad storms that are headed our way, even though they are wrong at times, even with all of the technology.

Finally, dads, I encourage you to be courageous with your sons. Don't teach them to be afraid of their own shadow. Raise boys that will become real men. Make memories by doing crazy and silly things; don't be so serious in life. Encourage your sons to take risks and to be afraid of nothing. Life is too short to worry about things that will probably never happen, and if they do, you will get through it.

Chapter 12:

Finding your North Star through Forgiveness

I think that every son in this world can look back at their childhood and see mistakes that their dad made in raising them. Even if they come from a loving family and both parents stayed together and never got divorced. If dads were honest with themselves, they would look back and have some regret in certain ways that they parented their children. But a lot of men are not willing to admit their mistakes to their children because, to some, it might feel like a sign of weakness or it might open up Pandora's box. Now there are the sons out there whose childhood and relationship with their dad was so bad that they could never see a day where they could forgive their dad for the things he has done to them or their family. I was one of those sons for a long time in my life, and even when I thought I had forgiven my dad, the root of bitterness would rise up from the depths of my soul, and then I knew that I hadn't truly forgiven my dad yet. So I would wrestle with that word, forgiveness, and try to deceive myself and act like I had forgiven my dad for the evil things he had done to our family and also to me.

Most families are dysfunctional to some degree. Sure, we all play that game that our family has our lives in order, but in reality, we are human, and none of us are perfect. I heard a funny saying that God gives you great friends to make up for the family he gave you. I speak for myself, but I feel that we all do this to some degree and look at other people's families and say, "Man, they're doing really well as a family." Then a few months later, you find out that the husband and wife are getting a divorce. This happened to me with one of my lacrosse players. His parents got divorced, and I thought that they had a really good relationship. None of us know what goes on behind the closed doors of someone's home.

When I finished Chapter 11, I thought I was done with the book, but then I started truck driving school in October of 2022. When I got to the school, all of the license plates of the trucks had my name on them, Leo137H. I was blown away. I looked up the angel reading for the number 137, and it basically said everything I was going through. It read the energies of all of the numbers, and they are a sign of new beginnings and fresh starts. It encourages you to break out of old mental, emotional, and spiritual patterns that no longer serve your highest good. Instead, it's urging you to embrace change with an open heart and mind.

Seeing the angel number 137 manifests a powerful reminder that you have everything you need to move forward with confidence. Your guardian angels are lighting your path and guiding you on your journey. The meaning of the angelic number allows you to have all the inner wisdom, courage, and strength that you need to achieve your goals and manifest the life of your dreams. It was crazy because here I was trying to get my CDL, which turned out to be harder for me than getting my pilot's license, and I struggled and failed my first road test, and it brought up all of my insecurities from my childhood. I knew that I had to write another chapter, and I was not done with the book.

While I was in truck driving school, my one instructor would always talk about a cone that he would reference while we were backing up into an area as the North Star. One day, while I was running and listening to worship music, I felt God say, "If you forgive your dad, you will find your North Star and walk in the destiny that I have planned for you." That day, I cried so hard like a baby, and I was literally screaming, saying to my dad that I forgive you and love you. I also felt that I should start thanking my dad for all the things he tried to do to show us love.

He would take us on vacation every year for two weeks to Cape Cod, in which he wouldn't make any money during that time because he had his own ceramic business. He built an ice rink in our backyard for us every winter so we could skate and play hockey. There were other things for which I thanked him that day. As I said in earlier chapters, my dad didn't have a great childhood, and as I look back, he did the best job he could to be a dad to us.

That day, I had a new appreciation for the things my dad did do for us to show us that he loved us, but I didn't see it as a kid. I experienced a deeper level of forgiveness towards my dad that day. Anger and bitterness will only destroy the person that is holding on to it. Have you ever been so angry at someone, and they came to you and said, "Your anger and bitterness towards me is killing me?" It's not affecting them, but it sure is disabling yourself and stopping you from reaching your True North or your North Star. Forgiveness won't change your dad, but it will sure change you. Forgive those that trespass against you. Trust me, I prefer an eye for an eye and a tooth for a tooth like in the Old Testament. Jesus was hanging on the cross, and he uttered, "Father, forgive them, for they know not what they do." I see that today—that we hurt people because we are hurt and broken people.

Everything that people do to hurt their loved ones, most of the time, is not done on purpose, but it is done just like Jesus said: they know not what they are doing. I screwed up my marriage, got a divorce, and hurt my ex-wife and my kids because I was a broken and hurt person and didn't realize the damage I was doing. It's like those people that are trying to find a perfect church to attend, and then they show up and mess it all up because they aren't perfect. Or you get that job that you dreamed of having, and then you start working there, and the employees are all complaining about how the job sucks, and then that perfect job you thought you were hired for is not perfect anymore. Depending on the level of abuse or neglect that you went through as a child will determine how deep those roots of bitterness are. I would think I let the anger and bitterness go, but there were still deep-seated wounds and pain that needed healing. We have to search deep inside our hearts to really see if we have truly forgiven. I can actually walk by my dad's picture in my living room, look at it, and say, "Dad, I love you and miss you." My wife and I met 14 years ago, and she can see how I have let forgiveness change me for the better. I still have a lot of healing to experience, and I don't think that I will stop continuing to heal until the day I take my last breath on this earth. I pray so hard that by reading this book, you can experience forgiveness and healing from your childhood.

I did end up passing my test and getting my CDL. I even got a really good job with JB Hunt right out of school, making really good money. I quit after two months of being on the road. It wasn't the right fit for me. Plus, I was not able to coach lacrosse, which was a huge passion for me. I know after reading this book you might say to yourself, "His poor wife," and you are right. She has to put up with my crazy self. Jack of all trades and master of none. The true saying of "a jack of all trades but a master of none" really has another part to it that my daughter told me: the last part of it says, "Better than a master of one." I realized that being on the road was not good for my family or my health. I have tried many jobs in my life, and I am OK with it. My daughter-in-law says when I talk about the jobs I have done in my life that you break out the rolls of paper that would have all of my jobs on my resume. But I hope it shows my kids that if I don't like a job, I am OK with walking away from it.

I am including in this chapter the story of how the slaves used the North Star to escape to freedom. The North Star is the anchor of the northern sky. It is a landmark, or sky marker, that helps those who follow it determine direction as it glows brightly to guide and lead toward a purposeful destination. It also has a symbolic meaning, for the North Star depicts a beacon of inspiration and hope to many. It means different things to individuals, populations of people, and cultures.

For African Americans, the North Star is as real as it is inspirational, and as spiritual as it is celestial. Many African Americans profess Christian beliefs and accept the details of the Magi as written in the first book of the New Testament. In the biblical sense, the Star of Bethlehem or the Christian Star appears in the Nativity story of the Gospel of Matthew, where the three wise kings from the East are inspired by the North Star to travel to Jerusalem. The star leads them to the Baby Jesus, where they worship Him and give Him gifts. Many Christians believe that the Star was a miraculous sign from God that foretold Christ's divinity.

My son told me that the North Star is a three-star system. Three in one, Remind you of something? The Father, Son, and Holy Ghost. Also, he said that by the time you see the star, it's light has traveled a very long way. In fact, various Christian denominations extend their celebration of the Star Prophecy well into the first week of January. The visit of the Three Kings to the Christ Child, the Nativity, Christmas, the Feast of the Circumcision, the Epiphany, and the Twelfth Night all proclaim the same time period that the North Star shone so bright in the night sky.

Another very important aspect of the North Star for African Americans is the indication of freedom. When enslaved people in the southern United States sought freedom from those who held them as captives, they devised ways to escape. As they fled from bondage, they looked in the night sky to give them direction on where to connect to the Underground Railroad headed to the northern United States and Canada. It was the constant guidance of the North Star that gave them the starting point and continuous connections on the journey northward. The Underground Railroad consisted of meeting points, secret routes, various forms of transportation, and safe houses along the way. Escaped slaves were assisted along numerous paths by free blacks, white abolitionists, former slaves, Native Americans, certain church clergy, and church members, all of whom played a role in helping African-American men, women, and children escape. One of the most famous and successful guides and conductors of the Underground Railroad was Harriet Tubman. Once enslaved, she perfected the navigation skills of following the North Star, the God-given glowing light that had enabled her to help others seek freedom in the north.

The North Star was also the name of an anti-slavery newspaper. It was started by Frederick Douglass, also a former slave who understood the depth of the importance of light and guidance. The name of the newspaper was quite befitting, as the publications gave references to the directions given to runaway slaves trying to reach the northern states and Canada. It focused on concerting the abolitionist movement and the fight to end slavery in America. The North Star newspaper was four pages long and sold by subscription at the cost of two dollars a year to more than 4,000 readers in the United States, Europe, and the West Indies. It had a most provocative slogan: "Right is of no sex—truth is of no color—God is the father of us all, and we are all brethren." Finally, the North Star has a very symbolic meaning for African Americans to embrace. Our historical leaders of the past have imparted such profound wisdom in the meaning of the North Star as a concept.

As we look within ourselves, we can seek our own internal compass that can guide us. We can discover and develop the gifts that we already have that can help us move forward as individuals and as a community. Isn't that what we all want to experience in our lives—freedom? Freedom in your life is truly only experienced through forgiveness. So unless you truly forgive your earthly father, you will never reach your true destination, and you will not find your North Star. I pray that this book will bring freedom from the chains of anger and bitterness that many have entangled themselves with because they feel justified in holding on to their hate. Remember, love covers a multitude of sins.

Made in the USA
Columbia, SC
30 June 2025